INTEGRITY

in a World of
Pretense

EARL F. PALMER

INSIGHTS FROM
THE BOOK
OF PHILIPPIANS

INTERVARSITY PRESS
DOWNERS GROVE, ILLINOIS 60515

InterVarsity Press is the book-publishing division of InterVarsity Christian Fellowship, a student movement active on campus at hundreds of universities, colleges and schools of nursing in the United States of America, and a member movement of the International Fellowship of Evangelical Students. For information about local and regional activities, write Public Relations Dept., InterVarsity Christian Fellowship, 6400 Schroeder Rd., P.O. Box 7895, Madison, WI 53707-7895.

All Scripture quotations, unless otherwise indicated, are from the Revised Standard Version of the Bible, copyright 1946, 1952, 1971 by the Division of Christian Education of the National Council of the Churches of Christ in the USA and used by permission.

ISBN 0-8308-1736-0

Printed in the United States of America ∞

Library of Congress Cataloging-in-Publication Data

Palmer, Earl F.
    Integrity in a world of pretense: insights from the book of Philippians/
by Earl Palmer.
        p.   cm.
    ISBN 0-8308-1736-0
    1. Bible. N.T. Philippians—Devotional literature.   2. Bible.
N.T. Philippians—Study.   I. Title.
BS2705.4.P35   1990
227'.606—dc20   90-45392
                                                                        CIP

16   15   14   13   12   11   10   9   8   7   6   5   4   3   2   1
04   03   02   01   00   99   98   97   96   95   94   93   92

For

Cathie Nicoll
Peter Yuen
Martha Chan
Donn Moomaw
Kay MacDonald
Howard Butt, Jr.
Sonny Salsbury
Thelma Enkema

You have each
in different ways
taught me the meanings
of integrity

Preface

The book of Philippians is a clear-headed and warm-hearted letter written by a man who knows who he is and a man who has not the slightest need to impress any reader with any theme but the living and good center of his faith.

The man writing is St. Paul. He sends this letter off near the end of a remarkable life in which he has lived through times of extreme danger and times of sheer encouragement. Paul has kept the faith, and this courageous faithfulness of his is one reason why the letter to the Philippians is so meaningful. The book has crystal-clear integrity in every sentence and every word.

As a pastor and teacher, I have often led studies and preached sermons from this letter of Paul's. Each time, the explosive and healing nature of the book has confronted me with new discoveries and new challenges.

There is something electrifying about the way people who hear and read Paul's words personally respond to what the text speaks, and their responses have become a vital part of my own journey of discovery. Now I have put down my own thoughts and responses to the Philippian letter in this book.

I especially want to express my appreciation to the people who have helped me as a writer: my two secretaries, Patti Nicholson in Berkeley and Helen Lower in Seattle; my typist, Mary Phillips; my editor, Ed van der Maas, who did substantial work on the manuscript and wrote the introduction; all the folks at IVP who helped get the book into print; my colleagues in ministry and the people in the churches of my life at Manila, Berkeley and Seattle. Most of all, my family—Shirley, Anne, Jonathan, Elizabeth and my mother and father—have encouraged me to keep up the work in this task, just as they are encouragers in every other way as well.

Earl F. Palmer

Introduction

Our lives often seem like overpacked suitcases bursting at the seams. In fact, we are almost always aware of being behind schedule. There is a nagging sense that there are unfinished tasks, unfulfilled promises, unrealized proposals. There is always something else that we should have remembered, done, or said. There are always people we did not speak to, write to, or visit. Thus, although we are very busy, we also have the lingering feeling of never really fulfilling our obligations.[1]

Does this sound familiar? Our lives are stretched to the limit but we somehow lack a clear sense of priorities or focus. We sometimes feel as if we were several people at once—and sometimes we wish we were, just to be able to keep up with the demands of our lives.

There are too many papers, magazines and books we think we should read, even though we couldn't possibly digest all the contents if we did manage to read it—we are on information overload. Most of us meet more people in a single day than a farmer in the Middle Ages would have met in a lifetime—we are on relational overload. The demands of our job don't leave us enough time to spend with our family; the demands of our job and our family don't leave us enough time to relax, reflect and take care of our spiritual needs—we are on demand overload.

Because there are so many things coming at us from the outside, we are not quite sure what the real core, the true center, of our existence is. Our Christian life vacillates between trying to aspire to perfection and true spirituality (although we really don't have much of a notion what that means) and profound disappointment with ourselves, with the church and its people, and even with God.

We are deeply aware that our lives lack *integration:* the various pieces just don't fit together. And because we lack integration we also lack its result, *integrity*. Integrity can mean two things. It means first of all "the condition of having no part taken away or wanting; undivided or unbroken state; material wholeness, completeness, entirety."[2] In this sense a building or a bridge can be said to have integrity. After the San Francisco earthquake of 1989, buildings and bridges had to be checked for structural integrity, that is, inspections had to be carried out to see if all the pieces of the structure still fit together exactly as they were supposed to.

But integrity has a second related meaning that is the meaning with which we are more familiar. This is integrity of behavior and actions or, as the dictionary puts it, "soundness of moral principle; the character of uncorrupted virtue, esp. in relation to truth and fair dealing; uprightness, honesty, sincerity."[3] This is the outward expression of inward integrity. Take a drawbridge. If its inward or structural integrity is impaired, it can no longer function with integrity, it can no longer do what it was designed to do.

Integrity means "wholeness, completeness, entirety." But we sense that we are lacking many things, we feel divided and often broken, we feel incomplete. That is how, all too often, we *really* feel. But that is not how others see us—because that is not how we *let* others see us. We compound the problem. Not only do we sense a lack of integration and integrity, we all too often lack the integrity to be honest about it. We pretend to others (and, if we do it long enough, to ourselves) that we have it all together, that we are successful people and good Christians while inside we are fighting a fierce battle to keep the strands of our life together and are crying for help.

It is strange that the word *integrity* occurs so rarely in the Bible—especially because integrity is directly or indirectly one of the major themes of the Bible. Perhaps we should be grateful. Because it occurs so infrequently it has not been trivialized by overuse. The great words of the Bible, such as faith, justification, redemption, and especially love, all have been used so much and are so familiar and comfortable to us that we *think* we know and understand what they mean when in reality all too often they are simply slogans or labels that hide our ignorance. We may be able to give a simple (or perhaps even a highly sophisticated) definition of them, but we have never had to struggle to understand what they really mean for us, here and now in the twentieth century. In fact, often these great terms have so much excess emotional baggage that we find it almost impossible to rediscover what they really are supposed to mean, practically and concretely.

This is why it can be very helpful to use a somewhat unfamiliar term such as integrity as a window on the Bible that gives us a new vantage point and a new perspective. It will not—cannot—reveal new truths, but it can help us gain a fresh and practical understanding of old truths.

Some five hundred years ago, Thomas à Kempis wrote, "What does it avail you to argue profoundly about the Trinity if you lack humility and thus displease the Trinity? . . . I would rather feel contrition than know its definition."[4]

The purpose of this book is not to outline a theoretical analysis and description of the concept of integrity. Rather, it is to show what it means to live as 24-hour-a-day Christians with integrity. And what better way to do this than by looking at a personal letter, written by the apostle Paul to a first-century group of believers who were remarkably like us in their problems and joys, conflicts and victories.

Paul did not write the letter to the Philippians as a treatise on integrity; and yet, that is in one way or another exactly what the letter is about, whether directly by means of exhortation or indirectly by means of example and illustration.

For Reflection:

1. Before you begin chapter 1, take a few minutes to write down your definition and description of integrity. (How does it affect you as an individual? You in relation to your family? to the environment? to your church? to your job? You as a citizen with political and economic responsibilities? Your recreation?)

Save what you write, so you can compare it later with your answer to the last question in this book.

THE ROAD
TO
INTEGRITY

I have been struck by the similarity between the dictionary definition of integrity, "wholeness, completeness, entirety," and the well-known phrase in James 1:4, "that you may be perfect and complete, lacking in nothing." I believe the apostle James is talking about integrity. But he makes it clear that integrity is *not* something we get all at once when we become Christians. The road to integrity is sometimes a rough road:

Count it all joy, my brethren, when you meet various trials, for you know that the testing of your faith produces steadfastness. And let steadfastness have its full effect, that you may be perfect and complete, lacking in nothing. (Jas 1:2-4)

Sooner or later every decision we make, every relationship we have and everything we feel secure about is tested. Even the words we speak to each other and the thoughts we silently ponder within the privacy of our hearts are tested sooner or later.

We think we have it all together, that our life is integrated and we can finally live with a degree of integrity, and then without a proper warning we are faced with some kind of threat to the stability of our life: we may lose our job, face illness, give in to temptation. Then the paradox of integrity happens. While we may think that our integrity is threatened by circumstances, it is precisely through the circumstances and dangers that threaten the integration of our lives that we come closer to achieving a life of true integrity.

A friendship that has been threatened by misunderstanding, gossip or distance and has survived will usually be stronger and more lasting than a friendship that is based merely on being comfortable with one another because we see things the same way and happen to live near one another. A marriage in which the partners have had to struggle with conflict and adversity and have overcome them is stronger than a marriage relationship that has never been threatened. When we have faced and survived the loss of our job and the sense of disintegration that comes with it, we have learned more about God's faithfulness, about ourselves, about our strengths and weaknesses, about our true values, and about the foundations that are durable.

What exactly are the kinds of threats you face? Is the danger obvious and violently blatant, with urban gangs that mark off sectors of the city as their own? Is the threat quieter and more gradual, such as the ache of unemployment and poverty? Is the danger internal, such as illness that threatens our well-being? The shape that peril takes will differ from person to person and from generation to generation, but testing is built in to life and is one of the ways we grow. People are often both a source of testing and a source of help through the testing. In fact, the most important lesson we learn when our stability and sense of having it all together are threatened is the importance of other people. We cannot go it alone, especially not in times of crisis.

Paul wrote the letter to the Philippians from Rome under circumstances that were intense and dangerous. Rome was a cruel and angry city at the time Paul wrote to his friends at Philippi. Nero had become emperor in A.D. 54 through murder and intrigue that had been actually sponsored by his ambitious mother, Agrippina. Britannicus the son of Claudius should have become emperor by right of birth as eldest son of the emperor, but he and his father were no match for Claudius' latest wife, Julia Agrippina.

Agrippina's son, Nero, was a teenager when he began his rule as emperor. The opening years of his reign were essentially peaceful and moderate because of the regency authority of Afranius Burrus and Lucius Annaeus Seneca, who together skillfully governed the Roman Empire in Nero's behalf until the young emperor, at age nineteen, made the decision that he intended to take full power into his own hands. From that point until Nero's death in A.D. 68 the Roman Empire descended into a period of terrifying cruelty and sadism sponsored by the personal depravity of Nero himself.

Nothing could stand in Nero's way or in any degree interrupt his own personal desires and his own lavish plans for Rome. He instituted daily gladiatorial contests in the arena; these became progressively bloodthirsty and decadent. Seneca wrote with dismay in his memoirs about these daily events at the Colosseum. After one such gladiatorial contest he wrote, "I felt as if I had been in a sewer." Nero became impatient with the moderation of Burrus and Seneca, dismissed them from their posts and finally arranged for their deaths. He murdered his own wife and finally arranged for the assassination of his mother, Agrippina. Her last words tell something of the horrifying story of Nero. "The one good thing about my death," she said to her executioners, "is that the womb that bore Nero is now dead."

Tacitus the historian accused Nero himself as the one who started the infamous fire in Rome in order to clear the way for his own grand plans for new buildings in the city. But what was to have been a small fire grew into a great conflagration and destroyed much of the city. Following this fire Nero, in the cynical style that marked his reign, blamed the small but growing band of Christian believers in Rome for the arson and meted out to them some of the most horrible punishments that have ever been chronicled in a civilized society. Tacitus describes the terror of that persecution:

And so, to get rid of this rumor, Nero set up as the culprits and punished with the utmost refinement of cruelty a class hated for their abominations, who are commonly called Christians. Christus, from whom their name is derived, was executed at the hands of the procurator Pontius Pilate in the reign of Tiberius. Checked for the moment, this pernicious superstition again broke out, not only in Judea, the source of the evil, but even in Rome, that receptacle for everything that is sordid and degrading from every quarter of the globe, which there finds a following. Accordingly, arrest was first made of those who confessed (i.e., to being Christians); then, on their evidence, an immense multitude was convicted, not so much on the charge of arson as because of hatred of the human race.

Besides being put to death, they were made to serve as objects of amusement; they were clad in the hides of beasts and torn to death by dogs; others were crucified, others set on fire to illuminate the night when daylight failed. Nero had thrown open his grounds for the display and was putting on a show in the circus, where he mingled with the people in the dress of a charioteer or drove about in his chariot.

All this gave rise to a feeling of pity, even towards men whose guilt merited the most exemplary punishment; for it was felt that they were being destroyed not for the public good but to gratify the cruelty of an individual.[1]

This is the city where Paul the Christian is imprisoned. At first his situation was tolerable. At the close of the book of Acts Luke tells us that the apostle Paul, upon his arrival in Rome as a prisoner in about A.D. 63, was probably under house arrest for at least two years and was during that time able to receive visitors "quite openly and unhindered" (Acts 28:31).

But by the time Paul writes his final letters from Rome (Philippians and 2 Timothy) his safety is very precarious and the conditions of his imprisonment have become harsher as the situation in Rome itself has become more chaotic and ominous. He gives at least two clues in the Philippian letter that this letter was written from Rome and that he was being held prisoner in one of the several prisons in that city, perhaps located near or actually in the vast villa at the southwest border of the Forum where the emperor himself lived.

First there is Paul's reference to the praetorian guard (Phil 1:13). This title is almost always a reference to the troops that were attached to the emperor and served as his personal guard. They were stationed in Rome and traveled with the emperor when he left the city.

The second clue is even more fascinating. Paul sends greetings from the Christians in Rome to the friends at Philippi and adds the surprising statement, "especially [from] those of Caesar's household" (Phil 4:22). Does Paul want to give his readers a clue as to which of the five principal prisons in Nero's Rome he is being held in? Is the apostle Paul at that time being held in the prison at Nero's Villa Vale? We cannot be sure. What is clear, however, is that this letter is written to the Philippians, not from the comfortable safety and stability of, say, Caesarea on the Palestinian coast, but from Rome itself, from the very heart of the decadent empire of Nero, and that it is written at the most unstable and, especially for Christians, dangerous period in that city's history.

Why has Paul written this letter? Paul is a "people person," and the personal element is always at the core of his letters. He cannot frame his profound ideological thoughts apart from the eternal Person and the ordinary people in his life. It is impossible to understand Paul the writer unless we see this fact clearly. Even his letter to the Romans, which shows us Paul most powerfully as theologian and philosopher, contains a chapter that reads like a telephone directory, with the names of people he knows and cares about in Rome.

I think this insistent personalism of Paul is what has made him so durable down through the centuries. Paul knows the person Jesus Christ as the center of his theology, not a Christ Idea or Christological symbol, but the real Jesus of Nazareth. Add to this personal center Paul's interest in people, some of whom we know by name—Epaphroditus, Timothy, Euodia, Clement, Priscilla, Titus and many others—and we have our most important clue as to why we treasure his epistles so much.

Paul and the people in his life are people who face dangers and the real threat of an empire enraged with power and careless wealth, an empire that menaces the struggling communities of the gospel; but these fellowships of believers are nevertheless growing, in spite of the dangers throughout the Mediterranean world of the Roman Empire. It is no accident that Paul is so people-oriented. True integrity involves being oriented toward others. How can we possibly integrate our lives, all the various elements in and around us, if we exclude the most important element—people? And this is why we love the letter to the Philippians, because it is written to and about people, people who are at risk.

The first reason Paul wrote this letter is the most obvious one because Paul mentions two names. Paul's friend Epaphroditus, who was sent by the Philippians to help Paul survive his imprisonment, has become ill and needs to return home. Paul writes the letter to accompany his friend, to help Epaphroditus with his reverse culture shock and especially, as we shall see later, his re-entry back into the circle of friends he must now meet again at Philippi. He also includes the news that another one of his close friends, Timothy, will soon arrive at Philippi. As always, Paul writes letters about real people in real places.

But the imprisoned apostle has another and equally personal reason for writing. He wants his friends at Philippi to be at peace about the welfare of Paul himself. This is a letter of assurance to them that their friend Paul is where he is supposed to be at this point in his life and that they should not be excessively alarmed about the fact of his imprisonment. One of the features of the personal style of Paul as a writer is revealed not only in his lists of names but also in his unaffected references to himself. Paul speaks often about his own feelings and experiences. We sometimes may get the feeling that he brags or complains, but perhaps the problem lies more with us: we find it so difficult to be straightforward and honest about ourselves that we cannot easily accept it in others. Either we play down our strengths under a misunderstanding of the meaning of humility or we play up our weaknesses to avoid personal responsibility. Paul does neither. He speaks with integrity about both his strengths and weaknesses, his failures and successes—and he can do so because he speaks from a life that is centered, a life that is integrated around his relationship with Jesus Christ.

A third reason for this letter is pastoral; Paul decides to speak frankly to his Christian friends about the threats the Philippians face from legalistic Christians who insist that the non-Jewish Christians in Philippi must comply with Old Testament circumcision practices. Paul also decides to pastorally address an argument in the church among some of its members, represented by Euodia, Syntyche and Clement (Phil 4).

But there is yet one more reason why Paul writes this letter, and this provides the vantage point from which we will look at the whole letter: Paul urges the Philippian Christians to live out their faith "worthy of the gospel." The Greek word translated "worthy" in the RSV is *axios*. Our English word "axiomatic" comes from this word. This word also carries with it in Greek the sense of congruence and equilibrium. Paul is urging a style of living that is congruent with, in keeping with, balanced by and dependent on the gospel of Jesus Christ. It is this integrity of life as a Christian woman or man that Paul advocates to the Philippians directly or indirectly in all of the letter. Philippians is therefore a book that speaks in many different voices about the meaning of integrity at a time of intense stress.

Each of Paul's reasons for writing this letter is relevant to the twentieth-century reader because Paul's philosophy of life shines through his words of counsel and his statements of hope reach beyond the time-space context of the world of the Philippians into our own. From the four chapters of Philippians we discover what this man believed, and it is the timeless core of conviction and the living center of each sentence of this Epistle that makes the letter durable and enduring.

Most of all, Paul helps us to understand what congruence and integrity in life mean, and that is no small achievement. So many things are not what they seem. I know of a person who withdrew $2,000 from a savings account because a young "official"-looking man had convinced my friend that he was a state examiner trying to uncover dishonest transfers of funds within the bank. But my suspicious depositor friend was suspicious of the wrong thing—it was not a corrupted bank that was illegally transferring his funds but rather the "examiner," and this pigeon-drop scam cost exactly $2,000. We live in a generation of hype and appearance, a time in which we must work hard at learning the ways to really value integrity, and that is the most persistent thread that appears over and over again in the fabric of this letter.

For Reflection:

1. Make a list of the things that worry you most, things that you see as threats to you, your family, the environment, your job, your church, your country.

2. "We find it so difficult to be straightforward and honest about ourselves. . . . Either we play down our strengths under the guise of humility or we play up our weaknesses to avoid personal responsibility" (p. 21-22). The question of strengths and weaknesses is important in this study. At the outset, spend some time thinking about your personal strengths and weaknesses. List them on paper.

It would be helpful to discuss your list with someone you trust (they may have some insights you don't have—it may not be comfortable, but it's worth it).

3. Do the same as in question 2, but this time think about your church's strengths and weaknesses.

CHAPTER 2

REAL PEOPLE
IN
REAL PLACES

P hilippi was a small city in the Roman province of Macedonia in northern Greece. We first encounter this city in the New Testament in the course of Paul's second missionary journey (Acts 16). Paul and his companions, Silvanus (Silas), Luke and Timothy, enter Europe for the first time through this military outpost village. In Acts 16:11-40 Luke tells of the amazing sequence of events that took place in Philippi. On their first Sabbath in the city, the four missionaries go to the riverside, where they find a "place of prayer." This place of prayer may have been an informal place of Jewish worship. (In Jewish practice there must be ten male founders in order to establish a synagogue, otherwise informal places of prayer are set up by believers.) Here a group of women have come together for worship.

One of these is Lydia, a businesswoman from the city of Thyatira in what is now western Turkey. She, a Greek woman, had been drawn to the message of the Law and the prophets of Israel, so that Luke describes her as "a worshiper of God." When she hears that the Old Testament hope, the prophesied Messiah, has been fulfilled in Jesus of Nazareth, she responds to the gospel: "The Lord opened her heart to give heed to what was said by Paul" (Acts 16:14). Here at the Riverside Bible Study Group are the first Christian converts in Europe: a Greek businesswoman and her family. "She was baptized, with her household" (Acts 16:15). This is the beginning of the church in Philippi.

But we know more about the beginnings of the congregation. In the city Paul meets a slave who is a priestess of Python. The English word "divination" in the RSV (Acts 16:16) is literally the word *pythōn* in Greek. The Python was the dragon that according to Greek mythology had been slain by the god Apollos. The priestesses who served as the oracles at Delphi were known as the "priestesses of the Python." Many people in the first-century Greek world believed that these priestesses were able to predict future events in their role as oracles of the Python at Delphi. Paul sets this slave priestess free from her cultic entrapment. The result is an immediate and furious response on the part of her owners and other citizens of Philippi, who demand that Paul and Silas be punished for being Jewish troublemakers who are spreading strange new teachings.

Anti-Semitism was widespread throughout the first-century world, as this incident shows: The city magistrates imprison Paul and Silas, unaware that they are Roman citizens. Luke and Timothy, who are Greeks, are not imprisoned.

In prison, according to Luke's brief account, Paul and Silas pass the time by praying and singing Christian songs. Then an earthquake breaks open the prison doors and its prisoners are set free. When the prison guard wakes up and realizes what has happened, he is determined to commit suicide. But at this dangerous moment in this unnamed guard's life he discovers the love of God, shown him through two of his prisoners. Paul and Silas, well aware of the stern disciplinary practices of the Roman military and also of the Roman tradition of committing suicide in the face of humiliation, have persuaded the other prisoners not to run away and by doing so they save the guard's life. This concrete experience of love breaks through the barrier of prejudice and fear, so much so that the guard comes to Paul and Silas and asks them to share with him the source of such a powerful love: "Men, what must I do to be saved?" (Acts 16:30). These are the unlikely beginnings of the church at Philippi: a wealthy Greek woman, an excited, enslaved mystical seer, and a badly shaken Roman guard.

It is hard to imagine a less homogeneous group and yet, because they share a common center and focus in the person of Jesus Christ, the church in Philippi grows in numbers and strength. It becomes a congregation with strong personal ties to Paul, even after the apostle leaves their city to continue his missionary journey. They are a caring church as shown by their response to the reports of the suffering of the Jewish church in Jerusalem. Paul will later, in a letter to the Corinthian church, tell of the overflowing generosity of the churches in the Roman province of Macedonia. Even though they were poor economically, they were nevertheless more than generous in their desire to share financially with the suffering people in Jerusalem who had been hit hard by famine and persecution during the years before the Roman destruction of Jerusalem in A.D. 70:

We want you to know, brethren, about the grace of God which has been shown in the churches of Macedonia, for in a severe test of affliction, their abundance of joy and their extreme poverty have overflowed in a wealth of liberality on their part. For they gave according to their means, as I can testify, and beyond their means, of their own free will, begging us earnestly for the favor of taking part in the relief of the saints—and this, not as we expected, but first they gave themselves to the Lord and to us by the will of God. Accordingly we have urged Titus that as he had already made a beginning, he should also complete among you this gracious work. Now as you excel in everything—in faith, in utterance, in knowledge, in all earnestness, and in your love for us—see that you excel in this gracious work also. (2 Cor 8:1-7)

This statement helps us appreciate something of the atmosphere in this church. The Philippian church must have followed the journeys of Paul with great interest. They would have known of his trips to Corinth, to Ephesus and finally to Jerusalem. During Paul's two-year detention in Caesarea (Acts 23:31—26:30) and the long sea journey to Rome (Acts 27—28), these close friends in Philippi would temporarily lose track of Paul's whereabouts, but finally word came back to them that Paul was now in prison in Rome and awaiting his trial before the emperor.

But Philippi and Rome are far removed, both in miles and years, from us at the end of the twentieth century. How can people and places that are so far removed from my time and place and people relate to my life today? Philippi is a long way from our street corners and from our daily experiences. How can an old letter, written to people who had no concept of the realities I have to face every day, teach me things that are really important for my life today? Distances of time and place are never as rigid and absolute as they appear at first. Each part of the human story lived out in one place becomes an analogy and mirror for each part of the story lived in another place and time.

I know business people like Lydia in my generation who are seriously disillusioned with the gods of their life, some of which may include money, success, power. These twentieth-century Lydias decide to explore the meaning of life. That decision brings them to a place of prayer in order to find answers to their questions. I know people like the Roman guard, with responsibilities that make unreasonable demands upon their lives, who have the kinds of radically overwhelming experiences that make them open up and ask deep questions of people they would normally ignore.

The "priestess" who tells fortunes on street corners is in my city an exploited human being in addictive bondage to a person or a chemical. Every generation has exploited people, addicted people, people knocked off their feet and unable to stand without help. The oracles at Delphi produced their convulsions and bizarre behavior through the laurel-bark narcotic. The woman at Philippi who "brought her owners much gain by soothsaying" (Acts 16:16) is an example contemporary to both Paul's time and ours. The tragedy of exploitation, the hideous distortions of drug addiction, the cruelty of every form of human bondage and slavery have been present realities in every generation. Time changes many of the *forms* in which human exploitation shows itself, but the essential need for human wholeness, integration and personal liberation remains constant.

In the same awful way, the fierce hostility that results when men and women see their power over any person or group of people threatened is a constant that remains, regardless of the forms or techniques of reprisal. In August of 1989 the government of Colombia attempted to systematically uproot the entrenched power structure of the cocaine cartel in that nation. The result was an intensification of bloody reprisals by the drug cartel against the government and citizens of Colombia who opposed it. In villages where the drug lords actually succeeded in intimidating local government officials they were able to put the government institutions, including local police and courts, to their own use in the punishment of reformists and anti-drug crusaders.

This is in principle no different than what Paul and Silas experienced at the hands of the Roman justice establishment in Philippi after they healed the priestess of Delphi. Because of racism ("These men are Jews") and because of the political and economic power of the slave owners ("When they saw their hope of gain was lost"), these two servants of Jesus Christ were beaten with rods and imprisoned. People who suffer because of racism and who have been wrongly punished by a system gone corrupt read the words about the founding of the church in Philippi through different eyes than those who have not had such experiences.

But even if we cannot relate to some things from personal experience, there is more than enough in Paul's letter to the Philippians which we can and should identify with—even though it is sometimes easier to keep things at the safe distance of almost twenty centuries so we don't have to face the unsettling implications and challenge of what Paul wrote.

By the time Paul arrives in Rome there is a dark cloud forming slowly but progressively over the Roman Empire in the moral deterioration of the whole political and social structure of the empire. Nero will arrange for the murder of Burrus and Seneca in A.D. 65, and he will personally rule in a reign of chaotic brutality unmatched in the history of any great city. Seneca, before his death, calls his beloved city of Rome a "sewer" of decadence and lust for cruelty as the people of Rome are drawn into the enjoyment of the vicious "games" that Nero himself orchestrated for the citizens' diversion.

Perhaps the Philippian Christians, living in a Roman military city, are more aware than other residents of the Roman Empire of the certain and progressive deterioration that they see shaping up within official Roman society. Whatever their reasons are, they decide to send one of their young church members, named Epaphroditus, to Rome with instructions to serve Paul in their behalf. Roman prisons were much like some today where prisoners need outside help from friends who supply food and other essentials if they are to survive for very long with their health intact. For example, prisoners in present-day Thailand must live on rice and thin fish soup for every meal unless they receive money from friends outside the prison which permits them to purchase fresh vegetables, fruit, eggs, meat and other food items.

So Epaphroditus was sent by the Christians at Philippi to ensure the health and survival of their friend and beloved founding pastor. But the young man Epaphroditus has become ill while at Rome—"for he has been longing for you all, and has been distressed because you heard that he was ill" (Phil 2:26). Therefore Paul decides that it is wise to send his friend home, with a letter that will turn out to be one of the very last letters of Paul (it seems likely that only 2 Timothy is written after this letter).

All of this means that we would not have this letter today had it not been for the kindness of the Philippian church in sending concrete help to the prisoner Paul. I have thought a lot about that. A local congregation, not by any means a leading first-century church, cared enough to want to help someone they knew was in need. Indirectly and unknowingly their act of kindness has had an impact on the church in every time and place because sending Epaphroditus—a relatively insignificant act in the overall scheme of history—resulted in the marvelous letter Paul wrote to them.

These speculations have convinced me that when I discover a need I should assume that the discovery itself is a gift. It is important to act concretely, swiftly and personally so that I can help where and when it is needed. We as churches and as individuals need to be either the Epaphroditus who goes to Rome or the ones who make it possible for him to go.

During the terrible days of World War 2, the Nazi S.S. forces deported Jewish residents of each of the countries of Europe under German occupation to the death camps of Auschwitz and Treblinka. In Budapest this systematic brutality was not as successful as elsewhere because of certain Spanish and Italian persons who cared enough to help arrange the amazing rescue of more than 10,000 Jewish victims. At the forefront of this courageous effort was an Italian businessman, Giorgio Parlasca, who lived in Budapest. Together with several others he personally shielded many men, women and children from certain death. One of those whom he helped is the Hungarian poet Eva Lang, who has remembered Giorgio Parlasca in her poem *Homage:*

> Our bodies bore the burden of a star
> But that man, who saved thousands,
> Made our burden lighter
> turned the yellow Star of Shame
> into a Decoration.
> That man, who saved thousands,
> Still lives, but he is silent.
> I must shout for him.

Parlasca was skillful in his shrewd use of a Spanish diplomatic passport that had by accident fallen into his hands. That skill, together with great courage, enabled him to confound the vicious extermination program of Nazi Germany in his bold strategy to hide people like Eva Lang who were forced to wear the yellow star to identify them as Jews.

Giorgio Parlasca's ministry of rescue began in a small way. He stumbled onto a crowd of people at the Budapest freight yard who were being forced into a German train. He noticed two twelve-year-old children and told them to jump into his car. This began his ministry of help. The large events of human history almost always have small beginnings. It is also true that not many people are willing to become this involved, but when one person takes the risk he or she will find that others will risk too.

When Paul was in need in Rome, where were the delegations from Ephesus, Corinth or Thessalonica? These larger and more influential communities of faith apparently did not decide to help. They may have had their reasons or perhaps their excuses. But the small church at Philippi wanted to help just as they had helped earlier in Paul's collection for the people suffering in Jerusalem.

They acted in a way that has become a model for Christian behavior whenever we become aware of a need, whether it is at a Budapest freight yard, in a shopping mall or on receiving news of a friend who is alone, like Paul in Rome. We cannot do everything and be everywhere, but the Philippians have shown to us how at least one fellowship of believers decided to act. We who live in our century are the benefactors of that young man Epaphroditus who served Paul. We profoundly benefit by the decision of the church that sent him to Rome and by the good sense of his wise, older friend who decided to send him home—with a priceless gift to all people and for all time—the letter of Paul to the Philippians.

For Reflection:

1. Sometimes small things can have major consequences. Look back over your own life and see if there were occasions when someone did something relatively small for you that had major consequences in your life. Was the other person aware of the importance of what he or she did? What is the significance of this for our dealings with others?

2. The church in Philippi started with a rather strange assortment of people from various socioeconomic, ethnic and cultural backgrounds. Could that be part of the reason for its lack in unity? In the U.S. today, most churches are relatively homogeneous, with members belonging generally to the same or similar ethnic and socioeconomic groups. Is it unavoidable that churches (and even denominations) will tend to become more homogeneous as time goes on? What are the *disadvantages* of being like each other?

CHAPTER 3

THE INTEGRITY

OF

THE CHURCH

Paul and Timothy, servants of Christ Jesus, To all the saints in Christ Jesus who are at Philippi, with the bishops and deacons: Grace to you and peace from God our Father and the Lord Jesus Christ. (PHIL 1:1-2)

W hen I went to college at the University of California in Berkeley I lived in a dorm with more than two hundred other men. There was a hall phone on each floor with hardly any privacy for a phone conversation. I remember very few phone calls. We met at cafés to talk if a conversation involved anything more than a work schedule change. And we wrote letters to the people in our lives to tell them how we felt and how we wanted them to feel about our feelings.

But the technology of communication has changed the way we express ourselves to each other. In the Berkeley of today many students have their own phones in their rooms, often complete with answering machines. One very communicative friend of mine has an answering machine on his car phone! It cheerfully announces, "I'm sorry but you have caught me at home; but leave your message at the tone and I'll call you when I'm out again."

What has happened in this communication explosion is that we have forgotten how to write letters. We talk and listen but what is missing is the one thing necessary in writing and reading: the communicative lag time that allows us to think about the feelings and ideas that are communicated. The result is a flood of impressions and a very high degree of immediate impact but little of the deeper etchings and the more complex, sustained ideas that cannot quickly be integrated into the flow of conversation or the sights and sounds of electronic communication.

Writing and reading letters provides opportunities for these more complex feelings and ideas to make their point and gain a hearing. This is why I try to win my college-age children over to the rapidly disappearing art of letter writing. The phone is a formidable competitor—except when it comes to humor, pathos, romance and the description of sights, especially when the writer encloses a photo. We are so used to "sound bites" and "factoids" that we are almost at the point where we have to learn all over again how to write and how to *read* a letter—in this case Paul's letter to the Philippians. We must read not just to get information but slowly and reflectively to understand the full range of what Paul is saying and what the implications are for us here and now.

As was customary in first-century Greek letters, Paul identifies himself immediately as the author, rather than waiting until the end to sign the letter. He also mentions Timothy, whom we as readers of the New Testament first meet in the opening sentences of Acts 16. Timothy, the son of a Greek father and a Jewish mother, was a close friend throughout Paul's ministry. Paul mentions Timothy no fewer than twenty-four times in his letters (his name also occurs six times in Acts). Perhaps Timothy was also the secretary who wrote this letter on Paul's behalf, since we know from other letters that it was Paul's method to dictate his letters to a secretary, who then wrote the necessarily compact, small Greek script on the very expensive writing surfaces used for first-century letters. Paul's own handwriting was very large, as he tells the Galatians (Gal 6:11), possibly as the result of bad eyesight (Gal 4:15), but at the end of a letter he would take the pen himself to write a final greeting: "I, Paul, write this greeting with my own hand. This is the mark in every letter of mine . . ." (2 Thess 3:17).

Paul describes himself and Timothy as "servants" of Christ Jesus. (*Doulos* may also be translated "slave.") It is the seeming paradox of God's reality, as opposed to ours, that true authority and true strength lie in servanthood. Jesus himself is the ultimate example for us: he became a servant of all and by doing so became Lord of all. We will come back to this in the next chapter. In the meantime we must see that Paul's authority derives from his servanthood. In our day, ironically, the term "minister" (from the Latin word for servant) has all too often become associated with the opposite of servanthood. Authority in the church, when separated from servanthood, becomes merely power. But when Paul describes himself as a servant of Christ Jesus we can test the truth of what he is saying by reading his letters and the story of his missionary journeys in Acts. Paul never claims to be either a perfect human being or a perfect servant, but with all his weaknesses and limitations, which he is the first to acknowledge, he has given himself to the service of Jesus and to the people Jesus came to save.

Paul writes to "all the saints." He uses the word "saints" or "holy ones" in the broader rather than narrower sense—not to describe people of exceptional spiritual standing and holiness, but as a description of the ordinary Christians at Philippi, along with their leaders. He does *not* say: "Warm greetings to the holy leaders (bishops and deacons) and secondarily all lesser other Christians at Philippi." Rather, the grand title "holy ones" is granted to the larger circle—to *all* who are in Christ Jesus at Philippi, the ordinary Christians, and their leaders, who are then also generously included.

The letter is not a general statement of theology but is addressed to particular people. This very element of particularity is an important feature not only of this letter but of the whole of the Bible. The fact of particularity is important theologically: there is no Christianity apart from the reality of faith as it takes shape in real people in real places. These are people who are called "saints" even though they have their problems and weaknesses, who move through the history of the world around them as a concrete physical presence, as an institution called the church.

There is no escaping the institutional, organizational aspect of the Christian faith when it is alive in people. As soon as people are in Christ by faith they discover men and women who also have faith in Jesus Christ and are drawn by the Holy Spirit into fellowship with these other believers. A fellowship comes together at Philippi that includes Lydia the businesswoman and her family, the slave priestess (now with her mind cleared), the prison guard and his family, and all others who trust in the gospel of Jesus Christ. When these people make even the simplest decisions about their common worship, their study of the faith, their service to others and their mission to the world, they are in the process of organizing themselves. Soon they will elect leaders and servants, bishops and deacons for the fellowship.

Paul greets the bishops (*episkopos*, "overseer") and the deacons (*diakonos*, "servant" or "minister"). These leader-servants are those who have a special task and ministry to perform on behalf of the people and the gospel. But the very heart of the description of the church at Philippi, the center that governs everything else, is the phrase "in Christ Jesus." This gathering of people in Christ Jesus is organized in order to be able to make the kinds of decisions that enable a young man named Epaphroditus to travel to meet up with Paul in Rome with collected gifts and with instructions for ministry from the fellowship.

There are Christians who wish for a form of Christian fellowship that is totally informal and noninstitutional. But these longings are not patterned after New Testament models because it is clear that the goal for the gatherings of Christians in the New Testament is a fellowship thoughtfully checked and balanced with just enough organization to keep it healthy.

Both the organization modeled by the New Testament church and the eternal mystery of the church that transcends any form of institutionalization are preserved by Paul's phrase "in Christ Jesus." Paul intends the order and institutional nature of the fellowship to be subject to Jesus Christ and under the authority of his eternal lordship. In other words, the Christian church is decidedly not a church simply because it elects or permits bishops and deacons and councils. In the most fundamental sense, the church is created by the mystery of obedience to Jesus Christ and our living, growing, day-to-day relationship with Jesus Christ that also enables us to continue being the church in the real world.

Nothing in the portrayal of the Christian church in the New Testament supports the idea that the church of Jesus Christ is a perfect fellowship that cannot and does not make mistakes. The New Testament churches were fellowships of ordinary people, and one of the most basic reasons that we have the New Testament letters in the first place is that those fellowships routinely made mistakes, some with minor consequences, others with very major consequences. "The Christian Church journeys through history in obedience and disobedience, in understanding and in misunderstanding of that lofty good that has been granted to it."[1]

The church is indeed human, but the church has come into existence by the divine action of God's grace in his Son, Jesus Christ. Therefore two things are always true about the Christian gatherings in the world, one an obvious but often-overlooked fact, the other a mystery. On the one hand, churches consist of real people in real places, like the Philippians at Philippi and Paul himself in Nero's prison. As real people they must face and make their own decisions about human existence with its temptations and problems, its joys and opportunities, because God in his wisdom has chosen not to take from those men and women who trust in his grace their real freedom to live as real people in real places. But on the other hand the profound mystery in the gospel is that these small groups of believers, here and there throughout the world of the first as well as the twenty-first century, are a people who have been called together by Jesus Christ. That they can be described by Paul as "holy ones" is the mystery that can never be blotted out.

Paul's description of the Christians as being holy and organized at the same time forces me to face up to a problem that I see all around me in the church to which I belong. I see the problem in others and in myself. It is a problem with two sides that appear to be opposites, even though they both have the same theological error at their source.

First, since the organization of the Christian church as an institution is so physically real and apparently understandable, I begin to imagine that the most important task for me as a Christian is to manage this institution and to make it succeed for God's purposes. So I put my organizational mind to this task, only to find that this becomes a destructive error because my mind becomes focused almost exclusively on the procedures of governance and the preservation of the institution of the church. I soon become a church leader primarily concerned with making sure that my plans (or the plans of my group) prevail in the church. I am organizing the organization and when my own expectations for that organization become too important to me, I have lost the vision of the mystery of God's presence in my own life and among these people who are God's people.

Organizations take on a dynamic life of their own, but that life does not have its source in the gospel of Jesus Christ. It springs instead from the organization itself. When this happens a Christian church or congregation of believers can become self-referential, self-justifying and in the end self-serving. The slogans may be gospel words but the focus is organizational and the motivation is power. This is the problem of the organizational captivity of the Christian. No one ever sets out to become an organization Christian, but it happens because it is easier to attend meetings than to pray and read the Bible. There is also the intoxication of power that has been as harmful to deacons and bishops as it has been to senators and mayors. The only cure for this problem is the reforming power of the gospel at work in my life.

The opposite threat to the health of the church is the danger of preoccupation with the celebration of the mystery of the church. I struggle with this problem, as I do with the preoccupation with the organizational problems. The danger of this preoccupation is a spiritualization of the church that results in an outlook that is so (apparently) spiritual that it will not allow the church's people to be *people*. The congregation of Christians becomes, in the mind of its members, more majestic and ideal than it really is. The destructiveness of this idealization may show up in an insistence on spiritual proof and spiritual explanation for every action and procedure of the community of believers. The spiritualization of the Christian church claims too much for the life of a fellowship of believers and as a result, when flaws appear, we discover how fragile and brittle ours has become. But our church is fragile because we shaped it that way. Our glorified image of the church leads to disappointment with the reality of the church.

The problem is that we cannot or do not want to see the difference. The argument between Euodia and Syntyche (Phil 4) is perceived as more disastrous than it really is because of the erroneous assumption that a truly "spiritual" fellowship would not have such disunity. Why not disagreement in a spiritual fellowship? The fact is that a spiritual fellowship may indeed have such arguments. The failure of Epaphroditus to stick it out in Rome, to be the servant he was sent to be, looms as a greater crisis than it really is in a fellowship that sees itself in ideal terms. We are tempted to read into his return all kinds of spiritual dimensions—perhaps even a direct attack of the Evil One—that are not appropriate and even profoundly harmful for every person involved. Some things just happen. And it is healthier to see them that way rather than to attempt too many explanations.

Both the captivity of the organizational-church realists and the captivity of the spiritualized-church idealists are risks that Paul's letter to the Philippians will face. We cannot expect more from the church as a corporate entity than from God's people as individuals. God does not make Christians perfect overnight; neither does he make the church a perfect institution. Rather, God's purpose is that the saints grow toward maturity and integration, and in the same way the church, which is both an organization and an organism, must grow toward integration. There will always be forces that fight against the integrity of the church. Any time we try to focus either on the church as an organization or on the church as a spiritual entity we distort reality and move away from the maturity the church is called to. There can only be one true focus for the church if it is to grow in maturity and grace. This is the very same focus the individual saints must be trained on: it is Jesus Christ at the center who keeps us real and alive. But we must watch closely that nothing removes him from the center.

Paul ends his opening greetings with the words "grace to you and peace." The standard Greek greeting was *chaire* (from the word for "rejoice"). But in his letters Paul replaces this standard greeting with what almost amounts to a pun. He changes *chaire* to *charis*, "grace" or "gracious gift." He links this with "peace." The Hebrew concept of *šālôm*, peace, is much broader and more inclusive than it is in either Greek or English. It means more than absence of war; it means "health," "wholeness," "integration," and I believe that it is this richer Hebrew meaning that Paul intends in this greeting.

"Grace to you and peace." As we shall see, there are people in Philippi who insist that all Christians should submit to the Jewish rite of circumcision. This must undoubtedly have created a tension between Greek and Jewish Christians, and it is very likely not an accident that Paul combines the richness of both the Greek and the Hebrew languages and cultures in his greeting. Paul's wish for his friends, Greek as well as Jewish Christians, is that they may know the gracious gift of God's love and the healthy integration that comes from God the Father and the Lord Jesus Christ.

For Reflection:

1. What is the relationship between servanthood, authority, power and leadership? How can one be a servant-leader? Does the servant-leadership principle also work outside the church (in organizations, in business)?

2. If it is true that the church should be both an organization and a mystery, how can this work out in the everyday life and activities of the church?

CHAPTER 4

DURABILITY

I thank my God in all my remembrance of you, always in every prayer of mine for you all making my prayer with joy, thankful for your partnership in the gospel from the first day until now. And I am sure that he who began a good work in you will bring it to completion at the day of Jesus Christ. It is right for me to feel thus about you all, because I hold you in my heart, for you are all partakers with me of grace, both in my imprisonment and in the defense and confirmation of the gospel. For God is my witness, how I yearn for you all with the affection of Christ Jesus. And it is my prayer that your love may abound more and more, with knowledge and all discernment, so that you may approve what is excellent, and may be pure and blameless for the day of Christ, filled with the fruits of righteousness which come through Jesus Christ, to the glory and praise of God. (PHIL 1:3-11)

P rayer is not a luxury or merely a spiritual exercise. It is the greatest integrative force we know. I don't mean the kind of prayer that asks for things to support our lifestyle or prayer to vindicate the rightness of our understanding but prayer that with an open heart and open mind brings the things of our everyday life, our problems and concerns, and the people in our life to God. This prayer bridges the gap we so often sense between our daily lives and our spiritual lives. It relates everything to God in the knowledge that he cares and understands. And often in praying about the things that confuse us and pull us in many directions, we find that in laying them out before God the relative importance of things becomes clearer, we remember things we had overlooked, and in that we begin to sense something of God's "grace and peace."

I know that when I pray at each meal and each evening the worries, the joys, the concerns that my mind is working on all converge into the sentences of my prayers. If there were a record of those daily prayers they would constitute a story of my life, of the life of my family and of the ways that I feel and care about the events of history-in-the-making as they happen around me and among the people in my life. Prayer contains a mixture of concern and gratefulness and sometimes the desperate cry for help. Our prayers are windows into our souls just as they are open doorways toward the Lord.

Paul prayed for many people. In every letter he writes, this remarkable man not only mentions the names of people for whom he prays regularly, but he also shares with his readers the content of his prayers. It is an important and helpful clue for our understanding of later themes in this letter to closely observe the subject matter of Paul's prayer of thanksgiving and his petitions to God on behalf of his friends at Philippi.

First Paul thanks God for all the memories he has of his friends in Philippi, memories that make his prayers for them joyful occasions. He is thankful for their partnership (koinōnia) in the gospel with him from the very beginning. The people in the Philippian congregation became Paul's good friends early in his ministry and they have stayed good friends; for this he is thankful to God.

After this prayer of thanksgiving Paul wants the Philippians to know a marvelous truth about themselves: God himself is at work in their lives to complete the good work that was begun in them when they first believed in Jesus Christ. The word Paul uses, *ergon* (work), has the meaning of work as a deed or action that shows itself in a concrete way. (In physics the term *erg*, a shortened form of this Greek word, is used to refer to a unit of work.) Paul's point is that God did something very concrete and real in our lives when we believed in him. God's "good work" is not something hidden, something that we will see only in the distant future, "at the day of Jesus Christ"—it is real and concrete here and now.

But it is an ongoing work. These ordinary Christians need to know that their faith journey is just that—a dynamic journey, not a static experience. The journey began when they trusted Jesus Christ as Savior and Lord and it continues as God is still dynamically at work in their present lives. Knowing this dynamic, moving fact about my Christian faith makes a very big difference in the way I look at my own life and the lives of other people. It means that things can change. Our experiences (and our opinions and feelings about them!) do not condemn us into immovable finalities.

One Tuesday I was standing in the parking lot of the First Presbyterian Church in Berkeley and a young man of about twenty-five walked up to me. Though I had never met him he knew who I was. He introduced himself to me as a graduate student in engineering at the University of California in Berkeley and asked if he could talk something over with me. In a very matter-of-fact way he said to me, "I've made some bad choices and those mistakes have caused harm to me and some other people too. Let me ask you, Pastor, what's the deal about forgiveness? How does it work?" He told me that he had heard a sermon of mine about forgiveness that had stirred up some questions for him. I will never forget that afternoon as we talked together about the meaning of forgiveness. I discovered in a fresh way through the eyes of this student the exciting dynamism of the good work of the gospel of Jesus Christ: There are no dead-end streets, no impossible debts. Jesus Christ is alive and he came to seek and to save those who are stuck in dead-end streets with impossible debts to pay.

Forgiveness creates new opportunities as the healthy result of repentance and of Christ's forgiveness at work in my life. It is this creative dynamism that Paul wants the Philippians to understand too. God alone is the absolute and final ground of being, and if this eternal God is at work in our lives to complete what has been initiated in our lives, then we must look differently at each debt and each dead-end street.

We talked in the parking lot, the engineering student and I, and we thought together about the powerful good news of the gospel that does indeed forgive and grant new beginnings. Forgiveness does not imagine away the harm that happens, nor does forgiveness create innocence as if our sins had never happened. The forgiveness of Jesus Christ is the event of reconciliation and redemption that sets free and brings resolution. These are better solutions, more realistic and more dynamic. This means that within the dynamic flow of the good and the caustic, the encouraging and the discouraging experiences, there is for each of us the companionship along the way of the God who is at work within and around our lives.

God is at work, bringing the pieces of our life together into a new whole. God's integrity ensures that we are moving toward our own integrity, even though we often feel that the opposite is happening. It is good occasionally to back off from our immediate situation and to look at how far we have come. We may be surprised at the changes we can see when we compare ourselves as we are now with the person we were ten years ago.

We tend to measure ourselves by absolute standards and find that we fall short of complete integration and integrity. And so we should: God's perfect integrity is the standard. But we forget that God does not use a magic wand to accomplish his work in us instantaneously. His purpose is to make us *grow* into maturity, into integration and integrity. When looking at another Christian we should not merely see where he or she is now in the Christian life, but rather from where and how far he or she has come. Our criticism of this person's shortcomings will often turn to praise for the work God has done in his or her life!

We are on a journey, and the concrete event that happened in us by faith will become more fully evident in our lives—until it is completed on the day when all of history converges into its final fulfillment in Christ: "The day of Jesus Christ." This term is used by Paul some twenty times in the New Testament. It also appears fifteen times in the Gospels (e.g., Mt 7:2). It is part of the eschatological language of the New Testament and looks toward the vindication of our Lord on the day of his final triumph. This means that in Paul's view human history moves toward that convergence point. History for Paul is delimited by the acts of God in Jesus Christ, who as Lord stands at history's three most important points: as the Word at history's beginning, in living presence at its center, and as ultimate fulfillment at its end. He is the one who will sum up the whole of the story of life and history.

The Christian journey is dynamic and that dynamic journey moves toward completion, toward the *telos*, the final completion at the day of Jesus Christ's ultimate triumph in history. Paul's use of the word *telos* is connected with the profoundly important Old Testament word *šālôm* (peace). This Hebrew word with all of its richly textured meanings of health and wholeness is translated in the Greek translation of the Old Testament, the Septuagint, by three Greek words: *sōtēria*, "salvation"; *eirēnē*, "peace" and *telos*, "end, goal." *Telos* is the word that Paul uses here: God "will bring it to completion."

It seems to me that Paul's first concern for the Philippians is this concern for their completion, their completeness and wholeness both as individuals and as a community. God is not only the true object of their faith. God is also the strong friend of their journey who has not left these ordinary Christian believers where they are at any one point of their life pilgrimage. God is at work in their hearts and minds and bodies to draw them step by step toward maturity and growth in grace.

When the profound significance of this prayer of Paul's really dawns upon me I realize that it is the Lord of life who is the true constant and not the various experiences or events of my life. This is something I need to be reminded of constantly because I and my generation take things too seriously. Here is an encouragement toward a more humorous and even mellow way of looking at life. The things that happen to me are the threads and colors that go into the total shaping of the weave. In all these things God is at work to complete and fulfill the final design, but that design is not finished yet because it waits for the day of Jesus Christ to be completed in its full glory. Paul's prayer does not imply that every occasion or separate part of the journey will be in itself good, but that the God who began the good work in us will complete it. In spite of the negative experiences along the journey, God's goal is our *šālôm,* our wholeness and peace, and God is at work to accomplish his goal in our lives.

Paul speaks warmly and personally to his friends: "I hold you in my heart," "I yearn for you." From these words they will realize how much he appreciates their loyalty to him throughout his imprisonments. Paul's next words show how he has integrated his theology and his life. He interprets these various imprisonments as a means by which the gospel has been *defended* and *confirmed.* This is not merely rationalization or denial, a way to put the best possible interpretation on bad circumstances, but a deeply felt understanding of God at the center of history and at the center of his own life. Paul also prays for the Christian character of the Philippian Christians, that their love will grow more and more with the fruits of righteousness. In each of Paul's letters we always find his strong concern for Christian piety and growth in grace. The prayer for the character of the Christian is fundamentally the prayer for integrity of lifestyle and behavior in these believers. When I reflect on my own generation of Christians in the world I realize how urgently contemporary Paul's prayer for the love that combines with righteousness is. It is a prayer for substantial people of integrity who are somehow not the "hollow men with head pieces stuffed with straw" (T. S. Eliot).

Tom Wolfe's novel *The Bonfire of the Vanities* has created a patchwork quilt of precisely such hollow people. One by one the characters in the story show themselves to be insubstantial and exploitative. No one can really help anyone else in the face of trouble because no one really cares that much over the long haul. Even parents, husbands and wives are too distracted by tiny, self-serving motives to make a difference as the people around them collapse. Only one character seems real and substantial: the young daughter, Campbell. She asks her father the big questions but her father "solves" those questions by evasions and lies. The novel creates a deadening ache, or perhaps for some more cynical readers a yawn, but underneath his story of New York, Tom Wolfe has focused a very small and weak flashlight on the bankruptcy of human power. His story and a thousand like it in modern literature and films reach out to our own generation with a longing for substantial people who care and believe and hope.

We live with the bonfires of the vanities each day, but Paul's century was also inflamed with power and he knows the emptiness that results from apparently limitless self-confidence. Human lives in his world were aflame with ambition and the desire for power in the apparently endless success of imperial Rome. Over against this ambition and power Paul puts a radically different power—love. It is what Martin Luther called "left-handed power." The "right-handed power" of the world is based on force and brute strength, whether military force or personal ambition. Right-handed power can always be defeated by a greater right-handed force. But left-handed power is the power of love, the power of forgiveness, the power of self-giving. Nothing can defeat it—there is no greater power in the universe. The cross of Christ is the greatest example of God's left-handed power. The power of Rome that put Jesus to death turned out to be nothing more than the instrument that ensured the victory of God's power of love and forgiveness.

In an episode of the television series "The Equalizer," a former

Cuban military officer charged with interrogating political prisoners describes why he quit and left the military and Cuba. He repeatedly interrogated one particular prisoner, held for political reasons and innocent of criminal wrongdoing. This man would not respond to threats and beatings, except by saying one thing every time he was interrogated: "I forgive you." In the end it broke the interrogator. He had met a power that was greater than any force he could bring to bear. This is, to the best of my knowledge, a fictional story, but it illustrates the point well.

But true spirituality is always practical. Paul does not merely pray for a love that grows more and more. Love must, according to Paul, be linked with knowledge and discernment. "Knowledge" is a firm understanding of the spiritual principles that are to guide them, that are to make this love practical. "Discernment" translates the Greek word *aisthēsis*, which is used only here in the New Testament and means "practical insight" in classical Greek. Paul thus prays for his friends that their love will be integrated with understanding and practical insight so that their love can be expressed in everyday life.

I was recently impressed by the comments of the distinguished pastor of the Young Nak Presbyterian Church in Seoul, Korea. When Dr. Kyung Chik Han was recently honored at a 50-year class reunion of Princeton Theological Seminary he answered several questions during an interview at the alumni banquet. At one point he explained the theological examination process for elders in the Young Nak Church, which with a membership of 50,000 communicants is the largest Presbyterian church in the world. He said that each prospective elder was examined in "Bible, Theology, Church History and Common Sense." Yes, of course, I thought to myself when I heard his remarks—common sense should be added to Theology, Church History and Bible!

The church in Seoul has borrowed their four criteria from Paul's prayer for the Christians at Philippi. Paul prays for a healthy dose of *aisthēsis,* that is, growth in common, practical sense, among the Christians so that they will choose the greater values over lesser values as they grow in the good fruit of righteousness. Paul has lived long enough to not be impressed by religious fanatics who redouble their efforts because they don't really see things clearly. Paul wants a sensible and thoughtful fellowship of Christians and he prays for this realistic common sense in their lives. Paul's prayer is for Christians who know that God is at work in their lives, who are growing in love with the fruits of righteousness, and who think clearly.

For Reflection:
1. We all know people we do not get along with. Think of one person in your church or family with whom you have trouble getting along. Is God at work in that person's life? Has there been change in that person's life since you have known him or her? How can you become an instrument of God's left-handed power in that person's life?
2. It is difficult to understand how left-handed power works in everyday life. Think of examples in your own experience. How can you (with God's help) put left-handed power to work in the family, on the job, in the church, in school, in politics?

CHAPTER 5

INTEGRITY
UNDER
ATTACK

I want you to know, brethren, that what has happened to me has really served to advance the gospel, so that it has become known throughout the whole praetorian guard and to all the rest that my imprisonment is for Christ; and most of the brethren have been made confident in the Lord because of my imprisonment, and are much more bold to speak the word of God without fear.

Some indeed preach Christ from envy and rivalry, but others from good will. The latter do it out of love, knowing that I am put here for the defense of the gospel; the former proclaim Christ out of partisanship, not sincerely but thinking to afflict me in my imprisonment. What then? Only that in every way, whether in pretense or in truth, Christ is proclaimed; and in that I rejoice.
(PHIL 1:12-18)

*P*aul knows that his friends at Philippi are worried about his safety, and he is anxious to put his situation in the right perspective for them. Paul is imprisoned in Rome, but he wants the Philippians to know that his imprisonment has not turned out to be a destructive blow to the gospel of Jesus Christ. On the contrary, it has in fact advanced the gospel.

Paul tells them that there have been two immediate and positive results of his imprisonment. The first is that he has become a famous prisoner among the soldiers who guard him. These elite soldiers of Nero's personal guard, the praetorian guard, know why he is in prison: It is because of the gospel of Jesus Christ. This is a marvelous thing to Paul. He has come to Rome as a prisoner from the distant provincial city of Caesarea because of a technical legal appeal, and as such the guards would hardly have given him a second thought. But Paul does not hesitate to speak freely of the real reason why he is there awaiting trial in Rome. The impression we get is that Paul shares his faith with those around him simply as a matter of fact, not out of defensiveness or with an I-am-right-and-you-are-wrong attitude, but out of the integrity of his faith. Paul rejoices in the fact that the reason for his being in prison is clearly understood by his warders so that his imprisonment is a continuation of his missionary journeys rather than the unfortunate end of his ministry.

The second positive result he points out to the Philippians is that most of the brothers and sisters in the Christian community have been encouraged by Paul's example to be more confident in the Lord. They have become *aphobōs*, without fear. (We get our word "phobia" from the Greek *phobos;* when the vowel *a* precedes a word in Greek it means "away from," "without," "no," as in the word "atypical."

What a remarkable and ironic development! Political and religious tyrants and systems of persecution achieve the opposite of what they intend to accomplish by means of force and terror. Rather than silencing the Christian community they only succeed in making it bolder and more outspoken, in driving out fear itself. With both Peter and Paul in prison, the emperor not only has failed to destroy this movement of Christian men and women but has instead given it new life and boldness. God uses unlikely instruments to achieve his purposes! Something similar happened in the recent history of Poland. The attempts at suppressing the Solidarity movement backfired for the communist government of Poland and more of its second-level leadership spoke out when its senior leader Lech Walesa was imprisoned than when he was free from harassment.

Yet all is not well. There are some who "preach Christ from envy and rivalry . . . out of partisanship, not sincerely but thinking to afflict me in my imprisonment." Who are these people who are preaching Christ with motives so unfriendly to Paul and his precarious situation as a prisoner? Paul does not actually identify them except to describe their motives with such terms as envy, rivalry, factionalism (partisanship) and insincerity. Are these people antagonistic Christians who disagree with Paul on some point of doctrine or practice? Or are they part of the general populace of Rome who are mocking the gospel of Christ by such street-theater events as preaching in jest? Our only clues are these few brief references by Paul. He does not choose to name any persons or groups so that his readers would be able to assign clear-cut responsibility. Instead of identifying those who seek to compound Paul's distress he surprises his readers by taking an entirely different approach.

It is one thing to see the positive side of difficult circumstances, such as losing a job or facing illness. It is something different altogether to be in a position where one's integrity is attacked and people are actively trying to undermine one's life work. How often do we see it happen that a Christian or group of Christians is more intent on proving the rightness of their own views or their own denomination than on preaching the liberating gospel of Jesus? They attack other people and denominations for somehow having it all wrong—even when the difference between them and those they attack is a relatively minor matter of doctrine or practice. Many pastors and laity have experienced this very thing on a more personal and painful level: people in the church who, convinced of their own rightness, attack their leaders for "being too spiritual, not spiritual enough, too dominant, too laid back, too loose, too structured, too disorganized."[1]

Paul's response is one that we can make only if our lives and our faith are truly integrated, if we know what is of ultimate importance. I don't think for a moment that Paul did not have to struggle with feelings of anger and resentment toward these people who made his life difficult. But his conclusion is that the preaching of the gospel is more important than the attacks on his person and integrity. He *rejoices* that Christ is being proclaimed and talked about, whether in pretense or in truth.

But how can people preach the gospel of truth from false motives? How can people who are wrong accomplish that which is good? Paul is deeply convinced of the surpassing efficacy of Jesus Christ, who can, as Paul's life shows, use the least likely people and events to achieve his purpose. Paul is convinced that Jesus Christ is able to break through even the most hostile settings in order to make himself known. Paul has seen in his own life journey as a servant of the gospel of Jesus Christ that often the apparently most negative situations have resulted in the most dramatic open doors. It was at Corinth, just when Paul was convinced that the Corinthian Jews would never give the gospel a fair hearing and he had made a hasty vow to avoid all future contact with Jews, that the ruler of the synagogue, a man named Crispus, became a believer (Acts 18). Similarly, when the prison ship that took Paul to Rome was shipwrecked off the island of Malta during a fierce storm, Paul had the opportunity to have a significant ministry to the crew of the ship and the residents of the island (Acts 27—28).

But what Paul and the Christian message now face in Rome is a more complicated danger because it attacks the very foundations: a deliberate distortion of both the message of the gospel and of Paul's ministry. The integrity of both Paul and his message are called into question. This is a graver crisis than the storms of the Mediterranean and much more potentially damaging. This more subtle calamity is harder to sort out and much harder to confront. Nevertheless, Paul is confident of the power of the essential truth that is found in Jesus Christ, and therefore he is prepared to ride out this present storm.

Paul's conviction is that over the long haul truth is stronger than falsehood and that the living God is able to endure pretense and distortions just as he has endured every other assault against him. In an ironic way the distorters may actually play a special role in preparing people for the gospel. Their garish and self-serving portrayals often put into relief the simplicity and straightforwardness of the true gospel, heightening the gospel's appeal.

In 1968 my wife, Shirley, and I took a trip with our children to the USSR. One of our visits was to the Museum of Religion and Atheism in Leningrad. On display was a heavy-handed Leninist-communist portrayal and interpretation of the history of the Russian Orthodox Church. The exhibit concluded its portrayal with the strong message of the inevitable superiority of Soviet Leninist communism over the superstitions of Russian Christianity and Judaism. The museum portrayed the Russian Christians as foolish, superstitious and morally bankrupt hypocrites. There were photos of priests who had been arrested for insanity or for various crimes against the people. I left the museum with a very good feeling about the future of Christianity in the USSR. I thought to myself, "With enemies like these who needs friends!" The average Russian secularist who visits such an exhibit has been prepared by the museum's message for the time when he or she will actually meet a Russian Christian, expecting him or her to be foolish, superstitious and hypocritical. But what happens when at the factory he or she meets a real, in-the-flesh Christian believer who is not foolish, who has a reasoned faith and who is morally forthright and honest? When this happens the very heavy-handedness of the state's attack on Christianity backfires and actually helps the cause of the gospel of Jesus Christ. Who is foolish now?

This is precisely the point of Aleksandr Solzhenitsyn's *One Day in the Life of Ivan Denisovich*. The cynic Ivan meets Alyoska, a young Christian who does not fit the carefully instilled, negative expectations about Christian believers which Ivan had been programmed to expect and find. And in that Nobel Prize-winning novel it is the young Baptist Alyoska who wins in the final scene of the story in his marvelous conversation with Ivan. It is Alyoska, with his face turned toward the light bulb reading the Gospels each night in the Siberian gulag, who has kept track of his sanity, his humor and his selfhood. When evening comes to the camp it is the young Baptist prisoner who makes sense when he talks, because the truth of what he found in the Gospels is more durable than the rhetoric of abuse that is sung out every day over the loudspeakers in the camp.

At the end of Ivan's day in prison he has those few moments of the soul when he can think a few private thoughts, and it is in those few moments that the Christian goodness of substantial hope makes sense to him. It is because of the Savior, who also suffered profound injustice, that in those few moments of quietness Ivan is able to weigh the differences between ultimate values and the various sounds of the day. At such a moment it doesn't really make that much difference that mockery and deception and falsehood were able to dominate the day with blaring forcefulness and apparent omnipresence. That strangely quiet moment when the camp is dark is in fact the most dangerous moment for all the propagandists and would-be re-educators of the soul. Ivan sees in Alyoska genuine hope and hears from Alyoska words that make sense when his young friend tells him the words of the "Our Father," the prayer that Jesus taught his disciples.

As I see it, it is the durable truthfulness for the long journey that is Paul's thrilling message to the Philippians in these sentences. He is alerting his Christian friends to trust in the durability of truth and the ability of God's truth to win at the moments that count most of all—not necessarily on the street corners of Rome, where crowds laugh with the thin running laughter of mockery as first-century talk-show hosts say hilarious things about Paul's gospel and the people of that gospel. Paul is not concerned about winning a victory at those jolting moments of derision and mockery, nor can he win the victory in Nero's arena, where the official policy of an empire has made the Christians and the Jews hated and persecuted minorities whom the public taunts with official endorsement. Paul is waiting for that moment when there is a pause of self-reflection, as when Seneca left the arena in grief and disgust. Paul knows that the gospel of Jesus Christ must wait for those moments of self-recognition when all of the hollow sounds really do sound hollow.

It is the kind of moment that happens, if only partially understood, in Tom Wolfe's *The Bonfire of the Vanities* when Sherman's daughter Campbell asks him, "Daddy, what if there isn't any God?" She is for her harassed father the only reference point that helps him to ask the Alyoska/Ivan questions at the end of the day. All of the others in his life are only concerned about Nero's parades and the endless dinner parties. The people on the way up the ladder of success in every generation are often so very busy keeping up appearances and maintaining and improving their positions that they do not dare to ponder Campbell's question. But sooner or later, in some unguarded moment, "life drops a question on your plate" (Eliot) and at that moment the parades and the entertainments of the arena are exposed for what they really are. It is at such a moment that the gospel of the living Jesus Christ will make sense to us.

Paul is willing to wait for those moments when the substantial realities outlast the superficial ones. This is why the strongest Christian witness is the simplest witness. It is straightforward, down-to-earth, earnest and growing faith in Jesus Christ that is the most powerful antidote to the ever-present but hollow sounds. Jesus Christ and the good news about his love for humankind are not fragile and brittle; they do not need special protection because light shines and love heals in the darkest corners and on the most confusing street corners where human beings must live and suffer. The gospel also makes sense in the joyous and expansive times when men or women make plans for the future to live out their dreams and hopes. The gospel is true and good wherever it is discovered. Since Paul knows this he is able to relax and trust. Time is on his side and he knows it. The Alyoskas of the USSR and Eastern Europe are no longer hidden away in the gulag as they were before the upheavals of 1989 and 1990. Their societies have found out for themselves that it was the loudspeakers of the State that carried the hollow sounds, and this has given each Alyoska in what once was the communist world a new chance to speak and to be heard. Nero will not outlast the truth of the gospel of Jesus Christ and Paul knows this even if Nero does not. Our integrity may be called into question and attacked, but the integrity of the gospel and God's integrity are the bedrock of reality.

For Reflection:
1. What are the differences between truth as embodied in doctrine and truth as embodied in a person's life? What is the relationship between the two? Can a person have incorrect doctrine and yet have truth in his or her life?

2. When we are faced with a disagreement in the church (or at home), we tend to accuse those who disagree with us of all kinds of intellectual or personality defects, such as dishonesty, stupidity, stubbornness, wrongheadedness or lack of spirituality. Can there be such a thing as honest disagreement in the church? If yes, how can we know whether the disagreement is an honest one or whether there are bad motives on either side (or on both sides)?

CHAPTER 6

THE GREAT CHOREOGRAPHER

Yes, and I shall rejoice. For I know that through your prayers and the help of the Spirit of Jesus Christ this will turn out for my deliverance, as it is my eager expectation and hope that I shall not be at all ashamed, but that with full courage now as always Christ will be honored in my body, whether by life or by death. For to me to live is Christ, and to die is gain. If it is to be life in the flesh, that means fruitful labor for me. Yet which I shall choose I cannot tell. I am hard pressed between the two. My desire is to depart and be with Christ, for that is far better.

But to remain in the flesh is more necessary on your account. Convinced of this, I know that I shall remain and continue with you all, for your progress and joy in the faith, so that in me you may have ample cause to glory in Christ Jesus, because of my coming to you again. (PHIL 1:19-26)

*P*aul does not present himself as a self-controlled individualist who, because of his special relationship with the Lord of his journey, has no need of the ordinary Christian friends at Philippi. Paul needs their prayers on his behalf and he cherishes those prayers. We have in these sentences a clear picture of Paul's understanding of the importance and authority that God has granted to human prayer.

Paul says that two things will combine to make the bad situation in which he finds himself turn out for his deliverance: the prayers of the Philippians and "the help of the Spirit of Jesus Christ." The word "help" in this sentence comes from a verb that has as its root the Greek word *chōros,* "choir" or "chorus." It originally meant "to lead a chorus," then "to pay the expenses for training a chorus," and by the time Paul wrote it had come to mean simply "to defray the expenses of something," "to provide," "to supply in abundance," "to choreograph."

This original root meaning of the word provides us with a marvelous and appropriate image for the work of the Holy Spirit in relation to our work of prayer. We can see the Holy Spirit as choreographing human prayer and his own work to make them work together in favor of this man who is imprisoned in Rome. This understanding of the "chorusing" ministry of the Spirit has greatly enriched my own need for and appreciation of intercessory prayer.

Prayer takes on a much greater significance and becomes part of a much larger reality when I fully comprehend the Holy Spirit's role in and through our prayers for other people. I am personally grateful for the good influence on my Christian journey of people who believed in this very active kind of prayer. I remember Dr. Henrietta Mears of the Hollywood Presbyterian Church, who was the mentor of many young pastors like myself early in my ministry. She often would say at some intense moment of a planning meeting, "Let's pray about it." Some of my greatest memories of breakthrough are of those times at Dr. Mears's cabin in Forest Home. We prayed together, we thought together with the Lord and we asked for help and for clarity of vision. And we experienced the choreography of the Holy Spirit!

There is a profound mystery here and I believe it happens as God draws together our concerns and requests and knits together vital elements of agreement. Paul believes this too. He describes here a wondrous partnership between the Philippian Christians and the Holy Spirit. These friends of Paul who have prayed for him are involved through their acts of prayer in a divine choreography or strategy that works in favor of this man for whom they pray.

When I discovered this mystery of intercessory prayer, my own prayers became more to me than merely strong expressions of wish and hope spoken toward God. I began to wonder about those experiences of prayer when my heart reached out toward someone who I knew was hurting. I wondered about the chorale of which prayer becomes a part in God's mysterious care for all those who hurt and who need care. We as intercessors make specific requests of God in our prayer. These requests are made in faith and according to this promise are chorused by God into a wholeness of God's intention. My own prayer is not diminished in its importance by this discovery—quite the opposite. I begin to become aware of a larger melody line, a more complete strategy. It is like being in a search party and finding in the forest other people who are also on the search for the one you care about.

I do not say that the discovery of the Holy Spirit as the great choreographer of our prayers means that I have more answers to all of the questions about prayer. Paul says that he *knows* that through the prayers of the Philippians and the help of the Holy Spirit the problems he is faced with—imprisonment and attacks on his ministry and integrity—will turn out for his "deliverance." The kind of deliverance that the Philippians intended and hoped for was a rescue of the apostle from imprisonment in Rome, so that Paul would be able to make more missionary journeys as the world's greatest ambassador of the gospel. Early in the Philippian letter Paul states his own prayerful expectation that such an answer to their prayers will indeed happen. But later on in the letter the words of Paul are not as focused on his planned return to Philippi but sound more like the words of a warrior who feels that his greatest contest lies ahead of him in the place where he is now.

What needs to be said is this. Both the Philippians and Paul had in mind a geographical and physical deliverance of the apostle Paul, but the historical evidence we have indicates that this rescue did not take place, even though they earnestly prayed to God for such a deliverance.

There are no easy answers to this dilemma for those who pray in faith, with concerns that are carefully, concretely, and spiritually stated, but who receive answers that are different than what they had asked. Paul never left his imprisonment in Rome. Scholars of the first-century period can conclude from all of the evidence they have that Paul's missionary journeys ended their course in Rome. This may have been a disappointment and a seeming denial of the request the Philippian church made in their prayers to God for Paul's deliverance, and of Paul's own personal prayers about his hope to visit good friends in Macedonia.

But the disappointment does not nullify the choreography or the choreographer. It adds one more ingredient to the whole mystery and practice of prayer. It is Jesus Christ the Lord who is the Lord of the answers to prayer as he is Lord in every other sense as well. This is expressed beautifully in a poem attributed to an unknown Confederate soldier:

I asked God for strength,
   that I might achieve,
I was made weak,
   that I might learn humbly to obey . . .

I asked for health,
   that I might do greater things,
I was given infirmity,
   that I might do better things . . .

I asked for riches,
   that I might be happy,
I was given poverty,
   that I might be wise . . .

I asked for power,
   that I might have the praise of men,
I was given weakness,
   that I might feel the need of God . . .

I asked for all things,
   that I might enjoy life,
I was given life,
   that I might enjoy all things . . .

I got nothing that I asked for—
but everything I had hoped for;
Almost despite myself,
my unspoken prayers were answered.
I am among all men most richly blessed.[1]

But we should note something else. The word Paul uses for "deliverance" is *sōtēria*, which is the same word that is usually translated "salvation" in the New Testament. It may well be that Paul used this word with an intentionally double meaning. We usually think of salvation as an event that takes place when we come to Christ. And this is true, but it is fortunately not the whole story. The work of salvation is "the good work" that God began in us and will bring to completion at the day of Jesus Christ. Whatever may happen, the prayers of the Philippians and the help of the Spirit will combine to further God's "good work" in Paul, the work of salvation from beginning to end—no matter what happens. It may mean physical deliverance or it may mean death.

Paul knows that he will not be ashamed, "disappointed" (the same word as in Rom 5:5; 2 Tim 1:12). Paul's hope is that he will have full courage so that the Lord Jesus Christ will be honored (praised) in Paul's body. When Paul introduces the word *courage* (boldness, openness) he shows us his awareness that the dangers are real and that the stress will be intense and threatening. What is very important for us to notice is that Paul does not spiritualize his aspirations. He does not turn inward to enjoy a personal, individualistic relationship with Christ while the world goes on around him. Rather, he sees his real life, lived in 24-hour cycles, and even his death as parts of the grand pattern of God's good work, designed to bring glory to Christ. Paul wants Christ's love to be shown in his physical-vocational-spiritual self.

He expresses this succinctly in the stirring phrase, "For me to live is Christ and to die is gain." This remarkable sentence is not framed in words of resignation or of fatalism. Instead they are the realistic result of the apostle's journey with Jesus Christ, his Savior, his Lord and his friend. He has entrusted the present to the hands of God and he also entrusts his future, whether it will be life or death, to those same hands, not grudgingly but eagerly because of the character and integrity of God.

Paul sees himself as the steward of his life. He knows that he has still unfinished tasks to do, and therefore there is no hint of a suicidal death wish in Paul. He simply trusts in Christ who stands at the end of his life as he stands at its beginning and at its center here and now. There is no false modesty in Paul: he knows how valuable his mind and vigorous leadership have been to the Christian movement and he realistically acknowledges that significance. We have here the healthy balance of a person who is realistic about the present and the future and who possesses that realism because it is founded in the revealed character of God.

During my ministry as a pastor at First Presbyterian Church of Berkeley I was honored to know as friends many truly great people. One of my favorite friends in our congregation was Ms. Dorothy Dod. She had been president of our United Presbyterian Women and also was a leader of stature in the community of Berkeley. Dorothy was struck with cancer in her late fifties. She struggled valiantly against the disease, but the battle was finally lost, and when she realized that the last days of her life were closing in on her she reluctantly agreed to hospitalization.

I remember as if it were yesterday a visit I had at the hospital with this remarkable woman. She was as alert and humorous

and interested in life and in people as ever. There was one character trait that everyone who knew Dorothy always loved or
feared: her crisp and definite, unambiguous way of speaking her
mind. Whatever the subject, Dorothy Dod said exactly what she
really felt, though never in a way that would harm. Her frank-
ness would at first shock the timid, but after a few seconds you
knew that somehow you felt better because of her clear, honest
and edifying way of speaking.

There was something I wanted Dorothy to know. I told her
that the way she was living her life during this illness was a great
inspiration to the people in our church and community who
knew her. I said, "Dorothy, your life is a real inspiration to me
and to everyone else." Her answer was wonderful. She said, "I
know it." That was Dorothy Dod in three matter-of-fact words!
She was not one to beat around the bush or decline these words
of mine. What I had said was true, and that was that!

I have often thought of Paul as a first-century Dorothy Dod
when it came to saying just what he thought and saying it without apology. He knows that his life and ministry have been a
great help to Christians in every city he has visited, and therefore
he simply says outright that he fully realizes that his ministry is
needed—and that is that. I think John Calvin in his commentary
on the Philippian letter has caught the central significance of this
sentence when he says,

> Interpreters have hitherto, in my opinion, given a wrong
> rendering and exposition to this passage; for they make this
> distinction, that Christ was life to Paul and death was gain. I
> on the other hand, make Christ the subject of discourse in
> both clauses, so that he is declared to be gain to him both in
> life and in death.[2]

Paul has both his life and his death on his mind, and he leaves each in God's hands. Dietrich Bonhoeffer stated in his own way the same double perspective when he wrote to friends in 1943, "We live each day as if it were our last and each day as if there were a great future."[3]

This fresh matter-of-factness of Paul in these sentences makes this part of Philippians very helpful and healing to us wherever we are on our life's journey or whatever our state of mind is. Paul's statement helps us make more sense of the present with its day-to-day stewardship responsibilities. The text also affirms to us that at the end of our lives we do not face an empty and inky abyss but the same Lord Jesus Christ whom we have known in our past and our present. We may pray for "deliverance" from our present situation, but we should remember that, like Paul, we should see the overarching reality of God's ongoing good work of salvation that will come to completion in the future, when we will "see him like he is." Whether this good work means physical deliverance or death, God knows what he is doing and he is bringing his work to completion. I need to keep my mind centered on Jesus Christ. Both my life with its responsibilities and my death as the earthly end of my ministry are in his hands.

Naturally I have both on my mind! We always think about death, sometimes too much, but we need to face our death in order to really live our life. One of the great enemies of true integration and integrity is the denial of our mortality. "Teach us to number our days that we may get a heart of wisdom" (Ps 90:12). There is so much to do and Paul's point is that our contemplations about death or about the complexity of life must not keep us from living. Paul is needed just as we are needed, and therefore he commits his contemplation to the Lord of his journey and then goes on. I know of no better way to live.

For Reflection:

1. "Prayer changes things." Is this true? If so, what does it change? Us? God? Circumstances?

2. Reread the poem on pp. 68-69. Go back over your life and think of situations or events that illustrate the truth of this poem.

CHAPTER 7

THE MEANING
OF
CONGRUENCE

Only let your manner of life be worthy of the gospel of Christ, so that whether I come and see you or am absent, I may hear of you that you stand firm in one spirit, with one mind striving side by side for the faith of the gospel, and not frightened in anything by your opponents. This is a clear omen to them of their destruction, but of your salvation, and that from God. For it has been granted to you that for the sake of Christ you should not only believe in him but also suffer for his sake, engaged in the same conflict which you saw and now hear to be mine. (PHIL 1:27-30)

N ow Paul comes to the heart of the matter when we think about integrity: "let your manner of life be worthy of the gospel of Christ." The word "worthy" *(axios)* means "corresponding, comparable, worthy." It is also the word used to express the concept of equilibrium. Paul talks here about a basic kind of congruence or integrity of life that is lived under the gospel of Jesus Christ. But the question for us is: What does he mean? Is he demanding perfection? Is that what *axios* means?

The key to understanding this mandate is the word *gospel*. He makes almost the identical point and in the same language in his letter to the Ephesians: "I therefore, a prisoner for the Lord, beg you to lead a life worthy of the calling to which you have been called" (Eph 4:1). What we have here is the basic evangelical ethic, the ethical distinctive of the New Testament. We are not told or warned to be good out of guilt or fear. Instead, we are first reminded of the gospel, the good news that we are loved, that God has begun to do a good work in us. Only then are we told that we must live out the love we have already experienced. This is exactly what John writes in his epistle, "Beloved, let us love one another; for love is of God, and he who loves is born of God and knows God" (1 Jn 4:7). Our only motivation is the good thing that has happened in us because of God's love for us.

This is what Paul is talking about to his friends, but we should make no mistake about it: it is an imperative! It is not so much a command to try to love as it is an exhortation to share the love we have received and to live under the influence of that good news. What adds a special wide-ranging scope to his imperative is the word the RSV translates "manner of life." Paul uses the Greek word *politeusthe,* which could be translated "your civic life," "your life as citizens." Paul addresses the Philippians as people who have inescapable individual responsibilities but who also have a common social responsibility to live out the results of the good news in their community. For Paul therefore the personal gospel is inevitably a public gospel as well. My colleague in ministry, Rev. Ronald Thompson, puts it well, "The Christian faith is personal but it is not private."

We are called to be a people under the gospel, a people who live in keeping with the gospel. This is my understanding of the intention behind Paul's use of the word *axios:* It is not a *perfectionist* mandate, it is a mandate to live out in our daily lives the *integrity* of the gospel. There is a big difference!

There are at least four threads that run through this mandate to live with integrity under the gospel. First there is the *realism* at the heart of the gospel that rules out every claim to our own perfection. Paul has no illusions about our human ability to perfectly live the will of God in daily public life. Earlier, in his classic letter to the Romans, he spoke autobiographically about his own failure to do the perfect will of God. In Romans 7:19 he describes his struggle: "For I do not do the good I want, but the evil I do not want is what I do." The gospel is marked by its basic realism about who we are: men and women who are sinful and who need God's eternal help. This is the gospel, and therefore to live in congruence with the gospel means living with this realistic understanding of what we are and what we are not.

This means that Christian integrity recognizes the ambiguities of the Christian man and woman. We are not small gods nor will we ever be gods, either small or large. This realistic recognition is what protects our discipleship from the false pathways of overstatement and glorification of our own piety. We are disciples who will always need the good news of forgiveness, and it is this recognition on our part that keeps us modest and teachable—and protects the world around us from the terror that results from people who perceive themselves as innocent and without ambiguity.

The most dangerous people we will ever meet in life are those who think of themselves as innocent. They see the evil around them but not within their own souls. Inability to understand our own ambiguity always produces self-righteousness and a severe hardness toward the people around us. The gospel of Christ does not shield me from facing up to my own mixed or even confused motives. Instead it enables me—in fact, requires me—to face myself squarely, knowing that Jesus Christ knows who I really am and that his grace is able to heal and restore in spite of those cross-purpose motives and deeds of my life.

I remember attending a Christian retreat when I was a student. The speaker was endeavoring to help us appreciate the wonder of our forgiveness because of the gospel of Christ. He said that the meaning of our justification was that God sees us "just as if I had never sinned." There was some truth in what he said, but part of it did not ring true. It implied that forgiveness produces a kind of newfound innocence in which I now can live, an innocence like Adam's before the Fall. But I *have* sinned, and my sins have caused real harm to people who were the victims of my sin. I also am the victim of my own various bad choices. Then I realized that the gospel of amazing grace offers forgiveness, not innocence. Forgiveness does not produce innocence; forgiveness produces reconciliation.

Justification sets us free from the terror of sin so that I do not stand alone before the power of sin but I have an advocate who stands alongside of me. Jesus is that advocate. He is the one who has taken my place at the moment of inevitable punishment. He is also the one who has conquered death, the inevitable result of sin. But this act of Jesus Christ does not make me innocent. It makes me safe, it sets me free, it resolves my sin, it calls me to gratitude, it fills me with love. It also makes it possible for me to find equilibrium, to find integrity. When I live my life under the gospel the first mark of integrity is that I have no false illusions about my own perfection. I am not shocked by human sin because the gospel has shown me my own sinfulness. This self-discovery, which I can make because I know that "there is therefore now no condemnation" (Rom 8:1), has a profoundly humanizing effect upon my life.

A second thread that runs through this mandate is that it takes us beyond the recognition of who we are to the realization of what we are to become. Each follower of Jesus Christ is called to stretch toward the "calling to which you have been called" (Eph 4:1). As believers we are called to follow in faithfulness the Lord of life. This is what Bonhoeffer called "the cost of discipleship:" "It is costly because it is the call to follow, it is grace because we are called to follow Jesus Christ."[1] The goal of the journey is to follow our Lord faithfully so that our lives will become increasingly congruent with his life.

The third thread in this colorful tapestry of discipleship is the dynamic quality of Christian existence that Paul spoke about earlier in his prayer for the Philippians (Phil 1:4-9). The Christian life is a life of robust and freeing growth. God is at work to complete that which has been started in the life of a believer, and this is the hope of even the most immature and faltering of the disciples of Jesus. No one needs to be permanently stuck in any one place. Because God is at work in our lives we are able to grow, and it is this dynamic nature of the Christian life that offers the hope that even the most persistent and addictive harmful patterns can be resolved and healed. This is why some of the most generous people I know are those who were once narrowly confined and grasping people who grew out of their harmful patterns as they grew in grace. I have friends in Alcoholics Anonymous who are available to stand alongside people in need because they have experienced help from others who intervened and from their own 12-step journeys that rearranged old patterns of isolating addiction to alcohol. Their new generosity with time and concern is the result of the dynamic nature of inner healing.

The fourth thread is really the foundation for the other three and the best of all. It is totally joyous because it is the gospel's heart and center. The gospel is the only truly good news in the universe because the love of Jesus Christ draws us toward goodness. Living under the gospel means living in fellowship with the Lord Jesus Christ, and that fellowship is the true source of congruence and integrity. He is the energy and the living presence who makes living under the good news totally good in the first place.

Paul follows up his mandate for personal integrity with a call for community integrity. We North Americans are individualists, and it is difficult for us to realize and accept that as Christians we cannot have true personal integrity unless we are also willing to work toward corporate integrity. Paul tells the Philippians [and us!] to "strive side by side." The word he uses is *synathleō*. *Athleō*, from which we derive our word "athletics," means "to strive for a prize," "to compete together." Paul uses this word in 2 Timothy 2:5 when he says, "An athlete is not crowned unless he *competes* according to the rules." Here he urges the Philippians to compete together, to work as a team, one in spirit and soul, without being startled by their opponents. If they do this, the result will be an evidence of their salvation and an ominous sign for the terror of the Roman Empire gone destructive with power and cruelty.

Paul sees three things that are evidence of the reality of the victory of the church at Philippi over its opponents: integrity, unity, and the ability not to be panicked by danger. These are essential qualities for any athletic team. Each player must not only have the personal integrity to want to do his or her individual best, but must also be a team player. Some players are more outstanding than others, but a superb quarterback can only be a star if he gets the protection and support of the rest of the team. Furthermore, before each game an NFL team will watch game films to find out how their opponents play and what they can expect when they go on the field. A good, well-coached team will not often be taken by surprise because they practice in order to know what to expect. And when a team that plays with individual and team integrity comes on the field and plays with conviction without allowing itself to be unsettled by the opponent's tactics, the opposing team may soon get a sense that they are going to lose the game. The integrity and unflappability of the team they are facing is "a clear omen."

Let us look now at each of these three evidences of the victory of faith. The first is the integrity of Christian men and women who are seeking to live their lives under the gospel. The very existence of human beings who know and keep track of who they are and who have the values of the gospel of Christ integrated into daily life is an impressive witness to the world of the power of God's salvation. Paul is not a triumphalist who sketches for us the heroic acts of super leaders. Rather, he talks about ordinary Christians who try to follow, in both private and public relationships, the results of the love and truth of Jesus Christ the Lord.

The second evidence is the unity of men and women who stand together in faith and who are soulmates in goal and purpose because of Christ. I once met the great missionary statesman E. Stanley Jones in the Philippines when I was a pastor there. I will never forget his words to a group of us, "You belong to Christ. I belong to Christ. We belong to each other." This fellowship of brothers and sisters who see themselves as teammates has a very powerful effect in every direction. Paul knows from personal experience that his brothers and sisters in Ephesus saved his life by preventing a foolish attempt he made to speak to a mob in the grand outdoor theater of Ephesus (Acts 19). These friends and teammates of his were able to play a helpful and strategic role in Paul's life as their collective judgment was wiser than his in that decisive moment. This is what teammates are all about, and now Paul encourages the Philippians to team together. The course of human history is too much a mixture of dangers and opportunities for privatism in the Christians' strategy, and Paul knows this from the experiences of his own journey.

The third evidence of victory for these first-century Christians (and, again, for us) will be their ability to carry on without the panicky disruptions of those who are too easily startled by the dangers of their century. Paul is *not* saying that an evidence of the victory of the first-century Christians or of Christians of the twentieth century over evil will depend on fearlessness in the face of danger. He is not speaking about fear and fearlessness, because there are many things rightly to be afraid of. In fact, the ability to experience fear is a God-given protection against genuine dangers. Meeting a grizzly bear face to face in an Alaskan forest should produce in us a legitimate sense of fear, as does standing in the path of a speeding car. But the word Paul uses, *ptyromai,* has to do with sudden fright more than with reasoned fear. It is the panic of a startled horse on the trail that acts hysterically because of some sudden fright. It is this panic reaction that Paul writes of when he tells his friends not to be startled. This word *ptyromai* is used almost exclusively in classical

Greek in reference to the sudden fear reaction of horses.

During the summer of 1987 I taught a summer school class on Philippians at Regent College in Vancouver, B.C. During one of the morning sessions we discussed this word, and during the coffee break a young man from Calgary sought me out because this word *ptyromai* had caught his attention. He was a rancher who worked with horses, and he told me that those who handle horses know all about *ptyromai* because it describes a horse that is "spooked" by something. He told me of races that are held in Calgary which test this very quality in horses as they run through a designed course that contains various jumps, obstacles and bridge crossings that ordinarily startle horses. The challenge of the race is to find the rider and the horse that are least easily spooked.

This is Paul's point. The gospel has a settling effect that results in men and women who do not startle as easily as they would have otherwise. All too often, we as human beings are unrealistic about the world around us and the dangers we face. Either we are unrealistically optimistic about ourselves and about the world, ignoring the awful reality of sin, or we are unduly pessimistic, ignoring the overwhelming reality of God's power, the left-handed power of his love. We often deny the reality and pervasiveness of the dangers by reducing them to a simple list of evils to avoid (from dancing to chewing gum) while ignoring the more subtle dangers that creep up on us unawares, such as materialism and striving for success.

The gospel calls for plain and simple realism. It is the realism of the gospel that produces its own brand of street-wise Christians who are not shocked by evil and its dangers when they are suddenly confronted by evil because they have found in the gospel the bedrock of reality. They are aware of the crisis caused by human sinfulness because they have faced it within their own lives.

Paul wants unflappable Christians at Philippi who will not err
either on the side of uninformed and naive optimism or on the
side of excessive fear and worry. Both of these errors in perspective result in people who are poorly equipped for the real dangers
that meet them on their journey. The one is panicked because
they had thought that this would be a tame and supervised path-
way without hazards. The other is panicked because they were
nervous to begin with—edgy and at the border of hysteria before
the trail began—because they expect at any moment dreadful
attacks against their safety. It is like the hiker who is too much
aware of the possibility of snakes along the trail. That hiker
walks too quietly and cautiously. But a little ordinary noise is a
very useful safeguard in snake territory. In each case, whether
we are overly optimistic or unduly pessimistic, we are ill prepared
for the journey where there are real hazards.

Paul presents these three evidences and then claims that these
three practical realities are evidence of the destruction of evil and
of our salvation. I do not believe that the context of the first
chapter points toward specific persons as the objects of destruction, but rather to the evil pressures and persecution of Nero's
Roman Empire. But Nero's power is less awesome when its
shock value is diminished and the limits of its power become
clear. In our day the evil pressures may not be as blatantly anti-
Christian as in Nero's Rome, but they may be all the more dangerous for being more subtle.

Paul's observation here is a true and accurate observation that
has been tested and verified throughout human history. It is a
fact that tyranny has lost much of its power when it has lost its
ability to produce the panic of immobilizing fear. Snakes, for
example, are not as frightful in reality as they are in our imagination. The possibility of a snake creates a sudden fright because

our imagination creates a greater danger than a snake can cause. But in the presence of a real snake the actual capabilities of the serpent are evident and the fear reaction diminishes. After all, a live diamondback rattlesnake can only strike one-third the length of its body!

As we grow into individual and corporate integrity our fears and our susceptibility to being frightened by evil will diminish. It is like a bridge that has structural integrity. Sudden wind gusts will not harm it—in fact, it is designed to withstand precisely those kinds of sudden stresses. But it all hinges on the center around which we integrate our lives: the radical possibility of a human being in relationship with the Living Lord. This center makes all the difference.

For Reflection:

1. Paul exhorts us to live our "civic life" worthy of the gospel. What does our civic life include? As citizens of a democratic country, do we have obligations that are different from those faced by the people of Paul's time? If so, what are they?

2. Individual integrity and corporate integrity are related and mutually supportive. What about individualism and corporate integrity? Can we balance the needs of the individual and the needs of the body?

3. The label "sin" is not exactly in fashion today (although sin is). Reflect on the statement, "Acknowledging sin is the gateway to liberation." Can you apply it to some current circumstance?

CHAPTER 8

ENCOURAGEMENT
THAT
LASTS

So if there is any encouragement in Christ, any incentive of love, any participation in the Spirit, any affection and sympathy, complete my joy by being of the same mind, having the same love, being in full accord and of one mind. Do nothing from selfishness or conceit, but in humility count others better than yourselves. Let each of you look not only to his own interests, but also to the interests of others. (PHIL 2:1-4)

T he integrity of faith demands that we give up the illusion of perfection and face the truth about the world, ourselves and the church. And this is what Paul does. There is one problem in the church at Philippi that now surfaces in Paul's letter. There are tensions in the congregation that cause certain members to oppose each other instead of teaming together in the unity of soul and spirit. Later Paul will name three people in the fellowship who are involved in the arguments that now endanger the unity of the church.

Controversies in churches are not new. They occurred in the New Testament churches, as each of the letters of the New Testament makes clear. I believe that we should understand this as both an encouraging and a discouraging fact.

On the one hand, it is unfortunate that very early in the life of the Christian fellowship there should have been the sort of conflict that threatened the effective witness of the Christian church in the world. Here in Philippi, for example, we have evidence of "in-house" struggles that use up the energy and time of the Christians. What a waste!

On the other hand, it shows that God uses that which is imperfect. This less-than-perfect fellowship at Philippi that must face up to some serious internal problems is the same fellowship used by God to send help to those suffering in Jerusalem, to be the witnessing church in Philippi and to send concrete help to Paul. In spite of the flaws of disunity and controversy, God makes use of such a fellowship, and he works with a church like the one at Philippi by encouraging Paul to write letters to them. As Karl Barth says, "There are no letters in the New Testament apart from the problems of the church." And even this letter, so warm and heartwarming, is a letter that must deal with a very real problem in the church.

One positive result is that the New Testament letters make it impossible for us as twentieth-century readers to idealize the Christian church and to create in our minds a fantasy portrait of the first-century church as a fellowship of faultless saints who because of their perfection had such a tremendous impact on their generation. When idealized portraits of the church of the New Testament era replace the accurate record of what really existed, the result will be dangerous, both theologically and historically, because it will make it impossible for us to build healthy discipleship models for Christian fellowships today. The church then becomes a divine ideal instead of a divine reality. Dietrich Bonhoeffer warned in his book about the church, *Life Together,* of the dangers of this kind of wish-dream idealism in defining and understanding the Christian church. These idealizations do not help us to really understand either the true situation among the first-century believers or their mandate and enablement—the mandate and enablement that are also ours today. "The Christian Church is not a divine ideal but a divine reality."[1]

Our task at the end of the twentieth century is not to try to be like what we imagine was a perfect and totally inspired first-century church or to try to learn special spiritual secrets which they knew but that have somehow been misplaced through the centuries. We have a better hope. The same Lord Jesus Christ who was Lord of the Philippian fellowship is Lord today, and we need his real presence and grace today even as they needed his grace and presence in the middle of their century. One more value of this first-century letter becomes clear when we recognize that the problems that proved to be troublesome for the Philippians in their time are problems that have their analogies and parallels in each generation. The people who make up our churches are very definite people who have definite ideas about almost every subject. This is not a weakness of the church—it is part of what makes the church actual and visible. But definiteness produces the colors that clash with each other as well as the colors that harmonize. In the same way positive discoveries of faith, hope and love in the first century have a positive analogy in our generation as well.

It is this shared humanity and the same living presence of Christ that make all of the letters of the New Testament contemporary documents of the Christian church in every age. For example, we know from letters written to the church in Philippi by Polycarp and by Ignatius sometime early in the second century that the Philippian Christians still struggled with problems of "factionalism" (as Ignatius called it) many decades after Paul wrote his letter. Divisions in a community of believers had a way of persisting then as they do now.

Now let us look at the way in which Paul decides to grapple with the factions at Philippi. As we saw in the last chapter, he begins by stressing the need for unity: "Stand firm in one spirit, striving side by side for the faith of the gospel." But Paul does not stop here. He knows that the Philippians are well aware of the problem and that they realize that disunity is wrong. He does not scold. Rather, he tries to move the Philippians away from focusing on their disagreements toward an appreciation of the good things they have experienced as a community. He uses words of encouragement and asks the Philippians to think about the meaning of those words.

He makes four statements beginning with "if." If these four things are true, if the Philippians have experienced them, then the church in Philippi has a solid foundation for unity and this foundation is what they must now focus on. The first of the four statements is the most important: "If there is any encouragement in Christ." The word translated "encouragement" is *paraklēsis*. It comes from a root that means "to call alongside" or "to come alongside." This is the same root from which the word is derived that is used for the Holy Spirit in the Gospel of John when Jesus promises the "comforter" (*paraklētos*), the one who will come alongside to teach us all that we need to know concerning Christ. The first question is, Has there been any concrete coming alongside, any concrete companionship, any encouragement in Christ? Before disunity reared its head, was there an experience of mutual encouragement in Christ, who is the only basis for unity?

Second, have they experienced any motivation and personal strengthening that had its source in mutual love? Third, have they experienced fellowship *(koinōnia)* in the Holy Spirit? And finally, have they experienced that warm affection that comes from their very deepest being and have they experienced any understanding and acts of mercy in the past? Paul knows that the church in Philippi has experienced all of these, and he asks the Philippians to remember the positive experiences of God's love at work in their own lives, experiences in which they have all shared. This positive exercise in remembering becomes the harmonious background against which he will draw the stark contrast with the controversy and negative anxieties that have made many members of the church highly critical of each other.

Here indeed is the apostle Paul as the originator of the theological and historical basis for the "power of positive thinking." Paul asks the Philippians to make a choice. Much like the psalmist who calls upon Israel to remember the goodness and faithfulness of God (Ps 103). Will they build on the concrete experiences of encouragement that they have received and experienced in Christ and among themselves, or will they ignore that foundation of encouragement in favor of the anger and destructive divisions in the church and the culture around them?

It seems ironic that the anger-producing memories that many people have of the church stem from interpersonal disappointment more often than from doctrinal disagreement. Someone has had his or her feelings hurt and that experience of harm-done-to-me becomes the major source of most church conflicts. I may not want to admit it, but if I am really honest I must agree. Paul challenges the Philippians—and us as well—to focus on the encouragements that we have found in Christ, so that we can be less terrorized by the discouragements and grievances we have so carefully cataloged against the people we know. He warns us as Christians against isolating ourselves because of real or imagined grievances and isolating ourselves because of our own self-righteousness. In this context he warns the Philippians against the way of conceit ("empty glory" is the word he uses here).

Paul advocates the oneness of love, and now from prison he urges his friends to choose that way. He is realistic in that advocacy, however, and recognizes that such a decision on the part of the Christians will be costly: they will lose the right to feel superior in relation to other Christians.

The decision in favor of the way of encouragement is, in Paul's view, the better way, but it is also the way that requires humility and a profoundly and deeply rooted concern for the sisters and brothers. The sentence "count others better than yourselves" (Phil 2:3) has been an awkward sentence to interpret because taken by itself it sounds very much like the sort of self-depreciation that few self-respecting modern men or women would ever take seriously. He has made use of a first-century expression that is best translated "Put others in line in front of yourself." When we understand this sense of Paul's statement we realize that he is not advocating the loss of self-esteem or self-respect, but in fact quite the opposite—he offers this behavior option as a proof of self-esteem.

Take a practical example from our own experience. Have you ever been in a supermarket to buy one or two items only to find that the express-checkout line is hopelessly long? You decide to wait your turn at a regular check-out line behind a person who has a cart full of groceries. At this point the person ahead of you says, "Hey, you go ahead in front of me, you only have a couple of things to buy." By all logic that customer, who has already spent almost an hour in the supermarket finding the things he or she needs, has the right to go ahead of you, who has spent only five minutes to pick up one or two items.

When that person invites you to go on ahead it is not usually a sign of low self-esteem but rather of just the opposite. Here is a person who is at peace with him- or herself to such a degree that the loss of a few minutes is seen in a larger frame of reference. People who can perform this small act of courtesy at a check-out stand are people who feel good enough about themselves to do you a favor. They focus on your interests for a few moments—not because they are weak but because they are strong. They are not preoccupied with narrowly defined justice and rights, but on generosity. Paul urges the Philippians and us to focus on the interests of others, on the needs of our neighbor, not because we are doormats or weak-willed, but for exactly the opposite reasons!

When we think of Christian love we often think of sacrificial kinds of things such as going to a cross-cultural mission field involving complicated mastery of sociology and languages. The truth of the matter is that here, as in 1 Corinthians 13, the great love-chapter, concrete love involves courtesy and tact and kindness—things that we can do in the supermarket as readily as in the church or on the mission field. And Christian integrity, while it sometimes will show itself in complex and difficult settings, is usually a matter of the small things in our day-to-day lives. Unity in the church would be easier to achieve if we would pay more attention to how we handle the small, everyday things in our life as a fellowship while keeping our main focus on the great things Jesus Christ has done for us individually and collectively.

For Reflection:

1. Reflect for a few moments on your church. What is the foundation for unity? (Social and economic similarity of its members? A comfortable agreement on doctrinal and social issues? A sense of being God's true church among all the other churches in your town?) Another way to look at this question is to ask what happens in your church to people who "rock the boat," who disagree on some doctrinal point or violate a dress code or simply ask too many questions.

2. We usually think of 1 Corinthians 13 as being a chapter that talks about *agapē*, divine love. But it is concerned too with our day-to-day life. Rewrite 1 Corinthians 13 in terms that can apply directly to a visit to the supermarket, or that applies to your work situation or your family.

CHAPTER 9

THE PRICE

OF

INTEGRITY

Have this mind among yourselves, which is yours in Christ Jesus, who, though he was in the form of God, did not count equality with God a thing to be grasped, but emptied himself, taking the form of a servant, being born in the likeness of men. And being found in human form he humbled himself and became obedient unto death, even death on a cross. Therefore God has highly exalted him and bestowed on him the name which is above every name, that at the name of Jesus every knee should bow, in heaven and on earth and under the earth, and every tongue confess that Jesus Christ is Lord, to the glory of God the Father. (PHIL 2:5-11)

Paul has told the Philippians how to live with integrity, both individually and as a community. Now he gives them the ultimate example of the fully integrated life, the only life ever lived with full and final integrity: the example of Jesus Christ.

But consider Jesus. His was not an illusion of superiority—he was truly and finally superior. He is divine. Compared to him, any claim to superiority we may think we have disappears—as does any claim to humility. Jesus shows that true greatness and true humility belong together, that they are integrated.

Paul begins by saying, "Have this mind among yourselves." The word translated "have [this] mind" *(phroneō)* has the meaning of intellect, perspective, point of view, a way of looking at life. When Paul begins to think about the way of looking at life that makes room for the interests and welfare of the person who is alongside you on the journey, he searches for an illustration to prove his point, and this brings the apostle to the high-water mark of the whole book.

Paul has offered some demanding advice to these Christians who have such problems with each other that a breach has already begun to show up in the fellowship. The apostle realizes how demanding this way of encouragement is going to be for these ordinary Christians, and therefore Paul now reaches down into the deepest source of motivation that he can find— the very revealed character of Jesus Christ himself who has modeled the ministry of encouragement beyond any limits we can imagine.

As I try to understand this greatest single Christological paragraph in all of Paul's writings in the context of the letter to the Philippians I believe that what happened is this: Paul wanted to show how Christ has encouraged us to care about others by his own way of humiliation on our behalf. Perhaps the apostle originally intended to offer one sentence to that effect. But what happened instead is that Paul's illustration, his model for encouraging the Philippians, began to enlarge in his mind as he wrote, so that what perhaps was to have been a simple sentence begins to extend itself into a song of profound descent and of majestic praise. The result is that the apostle has given the world the greatest hymn to the humiliation and exaltation of Jesus Christ to be found anywhere in the New Testament. What began as an illustration becomes a profound and astounding song of wonder at the personal and costly love of God, at the same time lowly and grand.

Paul begins with a portrayal of the person of Jesus Christ in the language of his eternal nature and true divinity as well as of his historical acts on our behalf as true man. Paul describes Jesus as being in the "form of God." The word for form is *morphē*, which means the essence of a reality, what Lightfoot calls "its specific character."[1] Jesus was equal with God. But he did not count equality with God "a thing to be grasped" *(harpagmos)*. This word is used only here in the New Testament. Its exact meaning in this verse has been much disputed, but the most likely meaning is something like "prize" or "booty." It can refer to either a prize that has already been obtained or a prize that is sought after. Either way, the point is clear: Jesus was willing to surrender his claim to equality with God.

At this point in the great hymn of the apostle we hear the powerful and costly word *kenōsis:* Jesus *emptied* himself, "not of his divine nature, for that was impossible, but of the glories."[2] He took upon himself the essential form (again the word *morphē* is used) of a servant/slave. And he was born in the likeness of a man *(homoiōma*, "likeness," indicates that Jesus was fully human). Paul now adds one more word of Christ's identification with us. He took on human form *(schēma*, outward shape). This Jesus, who has the essence of a slave and who is really like us as a human being and who even looks like us, is the same Jesus Christ who from the beginning is of the original being of God.

Paul has given us a portrayal of the uncompromised, total humanity and total deity of Jesus Christ. This Jesus is the one who has humbled himself and has identified with us by living as a human being. But he went beyond that. He identified with us to the point of voluntarily experiencing death. It is difficult for us to grasp the full impact of this because the death that Jesus faced was the death of total rejection and curse: the death of crucifixion.

But now we discover the greatest surprise of all: this humiliation becomes a victory. The low point of Jesus' human life turns out to be the high point of human history. In his voluntary humiliation on the cross Jesus Christ has won the victory over sin and death and the dreadful power of evil. Christ has broken the steel-like grasp of all three of these foes in the ultimate display of the surprising open-handed power of God. As Augustine sums it up, "Proud man would have died had not a lowly God found him."[3] Jesus has put us in front of himself and it has cost him his life.

But God has "highly exalted" him (Paul uses a luxurious compounded word by adding the prefix *hyper* to the already powerful word "exalt"). And God has given Jesus the Name that is above every other name. In the first century a man's or woman's name often signified his or her dignity or character. This was to some extent also true later, when people were often identified by their parentage (Johnson, "John's son") or by their occupation (Baker) or by the location of the family home (Green). But Jesus has the character and the dignity above all others in the story of names—not only on earth, which is the creation understandable to us, but also in heaven, which is beyond our understanding, and even in the shadowy realms of the places of death. In this great hymn we see the exaltation of Jesus Christ as the Last

Word, as the Lord over life and death, over heaven and hell. He reigns, and every tongue shall one day agree (the literal meaning of "confess") as to who he is. All of this is to the glory of God. Now we see that "the omnipotence of God and the love of God are the same thing."[4]

There is a profound poetic play on words within the structure of this hymn. In verse 3 Paul cautioned against conceit, *keno-doxa*, which literally means "empty glory." In verses 5-11 he shows the contrast between our empty glory and the greatness of Jesus Christ. Jesus Christ "emptied himself" *(kenoō)* and by doing so was exalted, to the glory *(doxa)* of God the Father. Here is the road to integrity. If we try to establish and prove our own glory, our own superiority, it will turn out to be empty and worthless. It is in the emptying of ourselves of any false claim to glory and praise from people (which is often nothing more than a vain attempt to convince ourselves of our own greatness in spite of the underlying reality which we know to be different) that God's power can work—"when I am weak, then I am strong"— and in the seeking of God's glory it is Jesus Christ who will be exalted.

Perhaps more than any other passage in Paul's writings, this marvelous hymn shows that Paul cannot talk about any major theme without relating it to Christ. For Paul, Jesus Christ is the foundation, the center, the focus that gives meaning to and integrates all of life. When he talks about ethics, about how we should live and act, he always goes back to the only motivation we have as Christians: the living Jesus Christ who makes it possible for one human being to have the resources to love another human being. Paul realizes that we cannot live by requirements of law or by trying to make up for previous failures in our lives. Trying to be good or to do better is motivated by fear or the threat of possible guilt, and such motivations have a very short-lived sustaining power. It is like a person who acts in a certain way in order to satisfy the social requirements of a particular circle of people whom he or she hopes to please: this person is motivated by fear of rejection by the group.

Paul's motivation for ethical behavior is not fear. It is grace, and the source of grace is the person Jesus Christ. The problem of our guilt has been resolved. And the way in which Jesus resolved the problem of our guilt, by refusing to claim the true glory which was his by rights, sets the example for us to have the same mind among ourselves by refusing to claim empty glory—to "do nothing from selfishness or conceit, but in humility count others better" than ourselves. Christ is therefore the fundamental starting point of Paul's total perspective. Karl Barth explained this in his comments on the great second article of Christian theology, "I believe in Jesus Christ the Son." "That is why Article II [of the creed], why Christology, is the touchstone of all knowledge of God in the Christian sense, the touchstone of all theology. 'Tell me how it stands with your Christology, and I shall tell you who you are.' "[5]

Paul does not assume that his readers will naturally build their lives on Jesus Christ as the foundation and center. He is aware of the many other powerfully tempting motivations for behavior in our everyday lives. The pressure to be accepted and welcomed into a special circle is as powerful a motivator in our lives as it was in Paul's century, because each one of us wants very much to be liked and accepted by the right people, the strong people, the pacesetters. This desire to be welcomed by a particular group of influential people poisons ethical behavior today as it has in every generation.

People have done reckless and cruel things to themselves and to others because of this one motivational hook that catches every one of us more times than we want to admit. We are familiar with peer pressure in high school. And there are the obvious examples of wanting to move up socially, to please the people who are in a position to help us move up the social or corporate ladder. But what about these same kinds of pressures in the church? How often do honest disagreements in the church escalate into major divisions because people align themselves with one group or another for the wrong reasons? How often do we ignore the need for fellowship of church members who do not quite fit our circle or clique?

The question is, How can we keep our integrity in places where such temptations confront us—even in the church? Sermons on integrity and reminders of the biblical commandments to speak the truth are no match for the persuasive power of the group of friends who want you to join with them in a particular attitude or behavior so that you can really become one of the group as an "insider." We need more than warnings or advice—we need the living center, the companionship of the man Jesus Christ who emptied himself for me and who is my friend here and now alongside me, twenty-four hours a day. There can be no unity, no unflappability, no life of integrity and congruence, no encouragement unless Jesus Christ is in our hearts as our living companion.

Against the glorious background of the example of Christ's self-emptying love stands, in stark relief, the emptiness of modern society. The winner of the Nobel Prize for Literature in 1980 was the Polish poet Czeslau Miloscz, who is professor emeritus of Slavic literature at the University of California in Berkeley. Professor Miloscz gave a speech in November of 1988 entitled "The Erosion of Faith in America." In this speech he reflected on the crisis in twentieth-century literature which he described as a crisis that is a result of the loss of faith in God in Western civilization.

One of the sentences in his speech made a very deep impression on me. He said, "The problem of the Western writer is that the Western writer is self-referential, and self-referential characters in stories or poems are boring characters." They do not struggle or come up against large values or laws or traditions that give them and their sufferings either rich humor or genuine pathos—whatever they say, do or think has importance only in relation to themselves and to nothing or no one else. T. S. Eliot made the same observation: "The hero/heroine in the modern story does not have a conscience, he or she only has nervous reactions." How interesting is it to read page after page about yet another odyssey of the nervous reactions of people who are doing their own thing, not because they feel strongly, but often "just because"? The characters are bored, sometimes terribly bored, and therefore they are usually boring. What makes a story exciting is what happens when the people in a story are really up to something that matters and they care about the outcome.

Casual wanderers who drift from street corner to street corner never bring excitement, except as they offer some possibility for contrast with other characters who really care. What is true of literature is also true of the everyday life of human beings. Self-referential men and women who have a minimal sense of discovery beyond themselves are alone with their own essential loneliness. But with only myself as a guidebook for the journey of my life I have no check or balance on my own instincts and immediate feelings. Even the laughter and humor are thin when the only point of the joke is myself—or someone else whom I mock because I am too weary to take him or her seriously. For every effort I make to rely, as a thoughtful humanist, on the inner moral voice of enlightened self-interest, the tragedy of the whole of it finally is this—I am alone because there is nothing else. Jean-Paul Sartre, our century's most substantial atheist, must have thought of this fact when he wrote in his final book, *Words: Reminders of My Life*, this line: "I only trust those who only trust God and I do not believe in God. Try and sort that out." Jean-Paul Sartre has found out the loneliness of self-referential existence, and he also has discovered that it is best not to depend on self-referential people at the important times.

Paul's century was self-referential like ours, and the appeal of the Jewish faith in the Greek world was its sense of the holy otherness of God and the fact that the Old Testament Law of Moses was *extra nos*, outside ourselves. The Law and the prophets offered a profoundly integrated and integrating reference point that made sense to the Greek businesswoman Lydia. Her openness was rewarded when she heard about Jesus, the fulfillment of that ancient law, from Paul, Silas, Timothy and Luke (Acts 16). The gospel about Jesus won her respect, and that gospel continues to win the respect of people today who wonder about durable values for life and a reliable truth around which they may integrate their lives. This is why Paul cannot bring up any subject and certainly not issues of morality, lifestyle or the meaning of everything, without finally breaking into the song of Philippians 2.

For Reflection:

1. Paul tells us to consider others better than ourselves. But how can I honestly consider someone else a better artist than myself if I know that that person cannot draw a straight line and is colorblind? Is Paul asking us to distort and devalue our abilities? If not, what?

2. What are some of the temptations and pressures in the church that move us away from unity, away from corporate and personal integrity?

CHAPTER 10

FEAR
AND
TREMBLING

Therefore, my beloved, as you have always obeyed, so now, not only as in my presence but much more in my absence, work out your own salvation with fear and trembling; for God is at work in you, both to will and to work for his good pleasure. (PHIL 2:12-13)

Have you ever had a moment in your life when you made such a total and all-encompassing discovery that you needed to do something about it? You are in love and you need to find someone to tell. Or you spent two days climbing Mt. Shasta and now you are back at the parking lot where your car is. You look up at the peak and you realize that you were on the summit of that 14,162-foot mountain. You find the nearest phone to let your Mom and Dad know of your success. Something like this happens when the applause finally ends at the last bow of a great moment in the theater. I remember when my son and I saw the musical *Les Miserables*. We were stunned and we needed time to talk about what had happened to us in that experience of music and song.

This is the way we feel after the hymn of Philippians 2. We sense in Paul's letter that he is deeply moved, as we are, by his hymn to Jesus Christ, and the words that follow make it clear. Paul calls out to his readers to seize this moment and to let the awe and the overpowering sense of the mighty grace of Jesus Christ permeate our lives.

We who are the recipients of that grace now want to make a response of our own. Paul tells us to "work out [our] own salvation with fear and trembling." Because of God's wondrous act in our favor we now must make God's act our own, make it practical here and now in our lives. His grace must work itself out through our lives. This sentence, which is a proclamation of freedom rather than the imposition of a burden, points out the intensely personal responsibility of working through the implications of Christ's salvation in all of the separate corridors and living rooms and small passageways of our lives. If Paul is community-oriented in his discipleship mandate ("Let your manner of life be worthy of the gospel of Christ," Phil 1:27), he is very person-oriented and deliberately individualistic in this sentence. The decisions and acts that integrate this understanding into all parts of your life and my life are decisions for which we alone are responsible.

Paul is fully aware of the urgency of this challenge and therefore he adds the words "with fear and trembling" (with *phobos* and *tromos*). *Phobos* is a common word for fear, from which we derive our word "phobia," and *tromos* means "shaking, quivering," especially from fear. We must be very careful to note that Paul is not telling his friends to earn their salvation by fearful and wakeful work and worry. There is no hidden theology of "salvation by works" now enveloped into the letter to the Philippians. Paul makes it quite clear that the miraculous gift of God's forgiveness originates from his grace and is prior to our response.

Paul combines his exhortation that we must work out our own salvation "with fear and trembling" with the promise that "God is at work in [us], both to will and to work for his good pleasure." This is what on the one hand makes the mandate possible and, at that, a joyous matter. But it is, on the other hand, the very thing that makes it a matter of great consequence. It is God who is at work, and that in itself causes us to quake.

In Paul's Greek sentence there is an emphasis that is somewhat obscured in the English translations. In New Testament Greek, the verb often is put in the first part of the sentence, but here Paul puts the verb last, which gives it special force. We could render his statement something like this: "Therefore, with fear and trembling, your own salvation, work it out—for God is at work in you."

Only I can make my salvation concrete in my everyday life; at the same time it is only God who can accomplish this in me. Paul combines the freedom of our faith and the sovereignty of God in these two verses in what seems to be a paradox. I am not on my own! But I do have the option to make this event of grace an event in my own daily life.

God is at work to carry out his gracious will, to make real in our lives what was the reality of Jesus' life. But we must equally be at work each day of our lives to spell out the implications. This means that we rest in the great fact that our salvation is a gift that all of our work and working could never achieve. Nevertheless we work because that salvation is so total and so complete that it demands a practical, everyday response from us.

This sounds like a contradiction. But it is not. The human experience of two people falling in love is very much like this "contradiction." There is the sense of rest in the experience of being a recipient of love and acceptance and commitment from another human being. But at the same time there is the good work that must inevitably follow as the two lovers make plans, busily tell friends, save money for future dreams and call up the church for a wedding date—all of this happens with not a little fear and trembling too! The work that these two lovers now take on is in no way an attempt to earn each other's love. That gift was given before the work begins, but the work is the natural consequence that follows the gift of love. What would really be odd is if there were one without the other. We now discover that what at first seemed like a contradiction is not a contradiction at all. "O God, Thou who art ever at rest and ever at work, may we be ever at rest and ever at work" (St. Augustine).

The salvation we have in Jesus Christ cannot simply be incorporated into our daily existence the way we handle some of the other "givens" of our lives, like a change in the schedule of the 7 bus that we usually take at 4:15 P.M. but now must take at 4:22 P.M. In cases like that we slightly adjust the routine of our day but probably with little or no fear and trembling involved.

But falling in love is a different matter. Hearing the news of the birth of our son or daughter is a radically life-altering event. And discovering that we are unconditionally loved by the Lord who has the Name above every name is the most radical discovery of all. When I discovered the love of Jesus Christ that discovery disrupted my life—but it also steadied my life because I was not only called to act, but I was met by the one who acts in my behalf.

The greatest integrating force in life is love—being loved for who we are, not what we are. And perhaps the greatest obstacle to inner personal integration is our inability to accept love, to allow ourselves to be loved by God and by people. Paul calls this the "good decision" of God. This is the meaning of the word *eudokia*. This is the word used in Luke's Gospel in the Christmas song of the angels which the shepherds first heard at night, "Glory to God in the highest and on earth peace, this is the good decision of God toward mankind."

For Reflection:

1. Explain in terms that a twelve-year-old can understand the paradox that we must work out our own salvation because God is at work in us.

2. Loving someone involves risk—the other person may reject our love and hurt us deeply. But there is also a risk in allowing ourselves to be loved, whether by people or by God—the other person or God may actually find out what we are *really* like and reject us. Do we really believe that God loves us? Think about how you can help others who have been hurt in the past to understand and accept the fact that they are fully and unconditionally loved by God.

CHAPTER 11

STRANGE POWER

Do all things without grumbling or questioning, that you may be blameless and innocent, children of God without blemish in the midst of a crooked and perverse generation, among whom you shine as lights in the world, holding fast the word of life, so that in the day of Christ I may be proud that I did not run in vain or labor in vain. Even if I am to be poured as a libation upon the sacrificial offering of your faith, I am glad and rejoice with you all. Likewise you also should be glad and rejoice with me. (PHIL 2:14-18)

There is a twofold focus in these words. First there is the clear challenge to make the experience of the salvation we have received real in our everyday lives because of Christ's love for us and to share the light of that salvation with the world where we live.

There is also the clear and definite promise of God's help and of his dynamic presence alongside and within all Christians who read the promise that goes with the challenge. The promise is found in three great words: salvation, light and life.

But Paul writes this mandate to the Philippian Christians, fully aware of the staggering odds that are massed like a vast and corrupt army against them, and Paul heightens the sense of an uneven match by his choice of words: the Christians he describes as blameless and innocent children, the opposition forces as a crooked and perverse generation.

I remember that when I first read the words in this paragraph I was struck by how unequal and badly matched the two sides appeared to be. On the one side Paul throws into the battle a band of warriors who are not to grumble and who are to be trusting, who are to be blameless and innocent—in fact, like children. I thought to myself, "Is this to be a children's army and is it placed over against a horde that is crooked (devious, twisted) and perverse (highly trained in evil ways)?" Is it like two teams, one playing by NCAA rules, the other playing by a different set of rules? Yet they are on the same field playing with the same ball. Who would want to play in such a game? It is like a karate match in which one competitor is instructed to abide by the traditional rules of karate and the other is told by his coach to injure his opponent with late hits and illegal moves.

Then comes the surprise: Paul tells his friends at Philippi that they have two weapons that are more powerful than the weapons of evil. And these weapons flow from the salvation they have experienced through Jesus Christ: light and life, the power of truth and the power of life. Now the match is a different story altogether!

If I were to pick the winner in a karate match I would choose the competitor who knows fully the "truth" of the event—the skill of karate—rather than the competitor who plans illegal and devious hits, especially if the one competitor is forewarned about, or discovers during the match, the crooked intentions of his opponent. The reason is that players who intend to break rules, whether in football or tennis, karate or cards, tend to be less skillful in the "truth" of the event since they depend on illegal moves to win. Once the honest athlete is aware of the presence of deception, the match is then tilted away from the crooked player and toward the player who really has the superior skills for the sport that is being played. Similarly, the advantage of evil is the short-term advantage of the surprise factor, but once the element of surprise has been eliminated the advantage returns to skill.

Paul has forewarned his teammates that as they face the contest against the powers of evil they will indeed be matched against all kinds of illegal plays. But it is not Paul's approach to train his team in more devious illegal countermoves, but to better train his colleagues in the "truth" of the game. Paul's strategy is wise and skillful. "The best defense against bad literature is a healthy diet of good literature" (C. S. Lewis). The best defense against a distorted thesis is an accurate and true thesis that will bear testing. The best defense against dishonesty is integrity.

This means that, even though we are denied by the truthful center of our faith the use of crooked methods and the weapons of right-handed power, we end up with the winning weapon of left-handed power: truth. Not only the truth of doctrinal statements and theological arguments, but truth-in-life: integrity. The strategy of integrity may appear slower but it is better because we never need to cover our tracks or remember the different stories we told to different people. Most of all, it is the strategy that is validated by the truth of God's character. Since the created universe is moral, this validation is no small matter!

We are not allowed to use deception for our own purposes or for the purposes of God. We therefore must always ask of ourselves as the fellowship of Christ if we are using methods appropriated from the opposition or from God. In our efforts to win the world for Christ, do we borrow fund-raising methods from Madison Avenue that are misleading and deceptive—although apparently successful? Do we replace the truth and integrity of the gospel with other criteria of success? And in the process do we surrender the weapons God has given to us, his "children in the midst of a crooked and perverse generation," the healing, hope-filled "weapons" of truth and integrity? This we must not do.

Added to the inner authority and power of light is the power of life—the greatest force in human experience. The word of life means that there is the possibility of forgiveness, of new life where previously the hope of life had been lost. Life is what the gospel is able to offer to a despairing and cynical generation.

When I was a pastor at Union Church of Manila in the Philippines, our home was on the same property as the church buildings and a large field separated the two locations. Our church council decided to transform a part of the open field into a parking lot and playing field. The land was prepared and the asphalt was poured and rolled into a fine parking lot. Every day I walked to the church across the parking lot and was pleased, especially during the rainy season, to be able to keep my shoes free from mud. It also was safer, since we had found three cobras in the field when it was still in its original condition.

One morning I noticed a few small elevations on the surface of the asphalt that looked like air bubbles forming beneath the pavement. For a while I wondered if there was perhaps a small pocket of methane gas trapped beneath our field that was now about to produce escape vents. But to my amazement it was not as dramatic as that.

One of the small bubbles finally broke open, and inside that fragmented hole in our asphalt pavement I found a very small, ordinary mushroom. Here was a fragile mushroom poking through a hole in our pavement—in fact, not just one mushroom but quite a few. How could it happen? It happened because the mushroom had something the asphalt did not have: life. Life is more powerful than concrete or asphalt, even though the small mushroom, when taken out of the pavement, is easily crushed.

There is life in the gospel, and it is this life that heals brokenness and hopelessness in human lives. Paul is fully aware of the harshness of the Roman world, but he has seen for himself the incredible power that the love of Jesus Christ has to create new possibilities in and through the apparently impossible situations of the first-century world. And therefore Paul is able to honestly make these promises.

But now Paul makes a statement that at first glance seems to be a sentence of grief, following as it does immediately after the great hymn to Christ and Paul's charge to the Philippians. "Even if I am to be poured as a libation upon the sacrificial offering of your faith. . . ." This is Paul's first suggestion in the letter to the Philippians that he may in fact not be released from Nero's prison as he had earlier hoped. Though he makes this obvious reference to his own possible death, nevertheless he reasserts his good cheer at thinking of his Christian friends at Philippi.

Paul follows the example of Jesus Christ with his own humble example. The life he has found in Christ is a life that transcends death, and Paul is willing to surrender his physical life in the service of others because he knows that the good work that God has begun in him does not end with death. Life will break through the finality of death, in the same way the defiant mushrooms broke through the asphalt under my parking lot.

For Reflection:

1. Find one or more illustrations, either from the Bible or from your own experience, of the principle that "truth-in-life" is ultimately stronger than any method based on falsehood.

2. Think of ways in which the church has, knowingly or otherwise, adopted secular strategies to promote church growth. (It is not always clear which of the two comes first!) After listing the obvious ones you have observed in other churches, take a look at your own church. By what means *should* the church grow, and how should the church win the lost at the end of the twentieth century—with full integrity?

CHAPTER 12

PEOPLE

I hope in the Lord Jesus to send Timothy to you soon, so that I may be cheered by news of you. I have no one like him, who will be genuinely anxious for your welfare. They all look after their own interests, not those of Jesus Christ. But Timothy's worth you know, how as a son with a father he has served with me in the gospel. I hope therefore to send him just as soon as I see how it will go with me; and I trust in the Lord that shortly I myself shall come also. I have thought it necessary to send to you Epaphroditus my brother and fellow worker and fellow soldier, and your messenger and minister to my need, for he has been longing for you all, and has been distressed because you heard that he was ill. Indeed he was ill, near to death. But God had mercy on him, and not only on him but on me also, lest I should have sorrow upon sorrow.

I am the more eager to send him, therefore, that you may rejoice at seeing him again, and that I may be less anxious. So receive him in the Lord with all joy; and honor such men, for he nearly died for the work of Christ, risking his life to complete your service to me. (PHIL 2:19-30)

P aul devotes the final words of this second chapter to two friends who will be traveling to Philippi: Epaphroditus, who will bring this letter with him, and Timothy, who will come sometime later. Timothy will come for a teaching and fact-finding visit, and Epaphroditus is coming home. The pastoral sensitivity of Paul in these sentences is a remarkable study in the skillful handling of a potentially embarrassing interpersonal situation.

His references to Timothy are straightforward. Paul wants Timothy to bring back news of the Philippian congregation, perhaps with stopovers at other congregations in Macedonia with which Paul had a special relationship. It is possible that Timothy's trip took longer than Paul expected, which would be the reason for Paul's later hurried letter to Timothy asking him to return to Rome before winter (the letter we know as 2 Timothy).

But Epaphroditus's trip home is a much more complicated matter, as the wording of the final paragraph of this chapter shows. Epaphroditus had been sent to help Paul. But now the young missionary is ill as well as homesick, and when he returns home he will need to face the members of the Philippian church without having completed the mission for which the church had sponsored him. We can easily draw the inference from the paragraph that Epaphroditus had been sent to stay for a longer time, but now the young man is too ill and perhaps too discouraged to stay.

Notice in the light of this situation how carefully the apostle Paul prepares the way for Epaphroditus to return home without losing face before his friends and family in the church. Paul takes the whole responsibility for the early return of Epaphroditus upon himself and then carefully adds descriptions of the character of this young missionary that still ring in our ears as a high tribute to a young servant of the Lord.

He instructs the church to "honor" Epaphroditus. This word has a rich Old Testament history in the Law of Moses. The Hebrew *kāḇôḏ* means literally to "weigh heavy." The fifth commandment instructs us to honor our parents, and now Paul uses this very word "honor" to describe the attitude the community should have toward a young short-term missionary. Paul wants the church to look at what Epaphroditus did, rather than what he did not do. Paul wants these friends to know the kind of fearless and courageous man that Epaphroditus has been. He is very careful to make sure that they do not treat him as the sickly short-term missionary who became ill in service to Paul. Paul loves Epaphroditus and he wants the church to love him too, and not only to love him, but to honor him as tough and courageous. This line gives us one more historical clue to the danger and the intensity of the pressures in Rome at the time of the writing of this letter.

Paul wants the Philippians to put on a parade for this returning hero who represented them at hard service in Rome. It was not a very pleasant task. It was very hard work and the thankless kind of service that takes a terrible toll. Paul actually tells the reader that Epaphroditus gambled with his life to be the servant that he was. Paul will not allow such a man to go unhonored. If the Philippians do not rightly honor him, if they allow him to quietly resume some place in the church community without really hearing his stories and experiences, they will have made a very major mistake and Paul does not want that to happen.

It happened in America after Vietnam when America's young men and women returned from a war that was not won and was fought in a very hard place far from home. There were no parades, there was very little thanks from an American citizenry that wanted only to erase the experience of an unpopular war and to get on with other things. We wanted to forget Vietnam, and so we quickly forgot the young men and women whom we had sent there. I believe our nation has paid a price in integrity and wholeness by that selective forgetfulness, and I am grateful that finally a proper monument to these soldiers of ours that we drafted into service and sent to an Asian war has been created in Washington. It came very late, but at last it is there as it should be.

I think the real test of a great Christian is how that Christian treats and cares for teammates who are somewhat down the ladder of recognized importance or who may not have lived up to our expectations. Paul in this letter scores very high by that test. For Paul this is not just a matter of harmony in the church or of protecting a young colleague from possible embarrassment. There is much more at stake. Paul realizes that the Christian church is not only an army engaged in a contest but also a fellowship in which people need to appreciate and honor each other. It is a matter of following the extravagant role model of the Lord of the Church who washed the feet of his disciples. Paul understands from his own personal experiences that Christians need to find ways to offer each other the extravagant friendship that makes each person feel their importance and their treasured value to us.

Paul experienced this when Barnabas put himself at risk by

offering the young Saul of Tarsus warm and supportive friend-ship. I know of no fellowship that was ever harmed by saying "thank you" too much or by showing affection toward each oth-er. But I am aware of many churches and families that dry up and become colorless and brittle because of a lack of wholesome affection among its members.

I am really challenged by Paul as a model of leadership in this passage. He shows affectionate concern for his young homesick colleague who now faces the strange glances of the people back home when they hear that Epaphroditus is already back after so short a time of service to the great apostle. I am deeply chal-lenged in my own leadership responsibilities by what Paul does just to assure and smooth the way for this young man.

As I read what Paul writes of his great respect for the coura-geous young missionary from Philippi, I wonder how I might be able to do the same kind of thing for the young Christian workers and friends whom I know. From my own experiences I know that encouragement and consideration always have a good effect and increase the deepest kinds of motivation. We do not have to be concerned that encouragement will produce pride. Pride is a cover-up sin of people who do not feel good about their relationship with people and with God and who therefore create myths of their own greatness. Prideful people, whether very young or very old, are usually people who are in the greatest need of an adequate source of approval and love.

But—and this is the key—the final approval has already been given by Jesus Christ, and because of the mystery of the Holy Spirit at work who assures us of God's love, this approval should also be manifested by Christ's people. This is a concrete example of the "good work" that God is doing in us, and it is one specific way in which we can "work out our own salvation"—by encouraging others, by looking at what they do and have done rather than at what we think they should have done.

We all know young people who have entered Bible college or seminary to prepare for the ministry. Some of them may drop out after a few semesters. Others finish their education but then, for one reason or another, do not go into full-time Christian ministry. The question is, are these students somehow failures in the ministry that God has intended for them, as people who set out to do what God called them to but fell by the wayside?

Paul would have understood. He would not consider the years spent in seminary wasted, just as the brief tenure of Epaphroditus is treated by Paul as both important and complete. His understanding of ministry was much broader, more confident in God's stewardship of our lives and careers. We are all full-time ministers of Christ, whether we are pastors, professors, artists, mechanics, housewives, or soldiers who guard the prisoners in Rome. It is God's choice whether he wants to use a seminary graduate in what we call full-time Christian ministry or in a "secular" calling. There are few things sadder than someone who is not happy as a pastor but who stays in the pastorate merely because he or she went to seminary and therefore feels that this is the only really devout option. We remember Epaphroditus—and especially Paul's evaluation of him!

For Reflection:

1. It can be just as harmful for a child to be pushed into responsibilities for which he or she is not ready as for the child to be kept from assuming legitimate responsibilities. How can we help a new believer grow up in Christ with integrity, without pushing too much or "babying" too much? In what areas should we expect (and allow) the new believer to make his or her own mistakes?

2. Is there a person in your church who is considered a "failure"? How much do you know about this person, about what he or she has gone through and why he or she has made certain decisions? Are there ways in which you can extend the "right hand of fellowship" to this person—as an equal before God, without condescension or violating his or her integrity? (Remember Phil 2:3b!)

CHAPTER 13

THE INTEGRITY
OF
THE SOURCE

Finally, my brethren, rejoice in the Lord. To write the same things to you is not irksome to me, and is safe for you. Look out for the dogs, look out for the evil-workers, look out for those who mutilate the flesh. For we are the true circumcision, who worship God in spirit, and glory in Christ Jesus, and put no confidence in the flesh. Though I myself have reason for confidence in the flesh also. If any other man thinks he has reason for confidence in the flesh, I have more: circumcised on the eighth day, of the people of Israel, of the tribe of Benjamin, a Hebrew born of Hebrews; as to the law a Pharisee, as to zeal a persecutor of the church, as to righteousness under the law blameless. But whatever gain I had, I counted as loss for the sake of Christ. Indeed I count everything as loss because of the surpassing worth of knowing Christ Jesus my Lord. For his sake I have suffered the loss of all things, and count them as refuse, in order that I may gain Christ and be found in him, not having a righteousness of my own, based on law, but that which is through faith in Christ, the righteousness from God that depends on faith; that I may know him and the power of his resurrection, and may share his sufferings, becoming like him in his death, that if possible I may attain the resurrection from the dead. (PHIL 3:1-11)

P aul begins the third chapter with the word "finally" and prepares us with that word for what we expect to be the conclusion of the letter. But Paul is a spontaneous writer and in every letter he writes, with the exception of the carefully crafted letter to the Romans, we feel the almost impulsive writing style of someone who is always ready to interrupt himself and his letter as he thinks of other concerns he wants to include. Paul interrupts what he intended to be the ending of his letter to the Philippians and decides to offer some further pastoral and theological counsel. We who now read the letter are thankful for Paul's impulsiveness.

Paul urges the Philippians to rejoice in the Lord, and then, without warning, he switches to the most negative statement in the epistle: "Look out for the dogs, look out for the evil-workers, look out for those who mutilate the flesh." But there is good reason for his sudden switch. As Paul tells the Philippians to rejoice in the Lord, he thinks of the greatest threat to the true and full enjoyment of the salvation of Jesus: legalism, the addition of requirements that need to be fulfilled for the gospel to become effective and specifically, here in Philippi, the requirement of circumcision to satisfy the Covenant Laws of the Old Testament. As if that ancient Covenant of belonging had not been already fulfilled in Jesus Christ alone. The apostle sounds an alarm and warns the Philippian Christians to look out for the "dogs." The term "dog" is always used in a negative sense in the Old and New Testaments. In the Old Testament the word implies chaotic uncleanness (see Deut 23:18). It is used by David in his angry words to Saul, "Am I a dog?" (1 Sam 24:14). The great Psalm 22 uses the word twice as a reference to the most villainous kind of attack on a person (vv. 16, 20). We know from the New Testament and other first-century sources that some Jews used the word "dog" as a crude and degrading description of non-Jews ("gentile dogs"). In Matthew 15:26 Jesus shows that he is aware of this crude racist practice.

But now, with sharp irony, Paul uses this word to describe precisely those who advocate strict adherence to Jewish practice and who would pride themselves on being supporters of the Jewish tradition! Paul is a colorful writer and his words always capture our attention and take us by surprise, as in his use of this angry expletive. But Paul's intention is to explain a very serious theological matter, not to shock his readers.

We know from the letter of Paul to the Galatians and from the record of the first ecumenical church council in Jerusalem (Acts 15) that a major question that troubled the early church was this: Is it necessary for a non-Jewish believer in Christ to be circumcised as a vital part of the journey of faith? That is, should non-Jewish believers first become Jewish, become part of God's covenant with Abraham, before that person can fully partake of the gospel of Christ?

Paul himself treasured his Jewish ancestry and legacy, and if anyone could claim to have the correct credentials for being a true Jew it was Paul. At one point Paul himself circumcised his Greek friend Timothy (Acts 16:3), but when Paul saw that this symbolic entry into the tradition of the Law and the prophets had become theologically distorted, so that some Jewish Christians in Jerusalem saw circumcision as an essential part of a person's experience of the promises of the gospel of Jesus Christ, Paul stood firm and refused to allow the circumcision of another Greek friend, Titus (Gal 2:1-5). He explains in Galatians that the reason for his rejection of the need of circumcision in the case of Titus was that such an act would have distorted the integrity of the gospel.

Therefore Paul and Barnabas and the church at Antioch requested a meeting of the church leaders in Jerusalem. At that meeting the question was settled by the early Christian church. The non-Jewish believer does not need to become a Jew in order to know Christ's grace. Peter spoke movingly at the close of that historical meeting: "We believe that we shall be saved through the grace of the Lord Jesus, just as they [the Gentiles] will. . . . Therefore my judgment is that we should not trouble those of the Gentiles who turn to God" (Acts 15:11, 19).

But bad theory and bad practice have a long and persistent staying power—even when the church has decided in favor of the greater truth. This is why the church in every generation needs the purifying, reforming and correcting ministry of sound teaching and sound doctrine. We are always in danger of going astray, and usually our going astray is motivated by half the truth proclaimed or by a theory that appears more reverent and more devout than what others in the church are teaching. False teaching is often very difficult to sort out because it has an aura of sincere discipleship about it.

The false teachers in Philippi exhorted the male Christians to prove their real devotion to the Lord by an act of discipleship that is more demanding and therefore, they argued, more "spiritual" than the apparently "easy" gospel that they had heard from Paul. These teachers may have accused Paul of being soft and a compromiser—and they could back it up by quoting Scripture! They were able to quote Old Testament texts that tell of the sign of circumcision and its importance as the true sign of the covenant God made with Abraham.

What are ordinary Christians supposed to do in the face of these specialized evangelists who have such an apparently well-reasoned and biblically founded teaching? We as twentieth-century Christians must face this challenge as much as the people at Philippi. We meet advocates of new religious movements who remind us of our own shortcomings, and in most instances these new-movement teachers display their evidence so effectively that their arguments against the ordinary Christians and against our churches may be very persuasive. They may emphasize the divisions within the church and claim that this new movement has new light or offers a new unification of Christianity. Or they may stress the powerlessness of Christians and promise sources of new power only available within the new patterns and through the methods of the new movement. Or we may be reminded of the hypocrisy of churches and Christians in their lack of caring for the poor, and therefore it might be argued that only advocacy for the poor is a test of real discipleship that creates the possibility of genuine redemption.

The list is a long and complex one today just as it was in the first century. On the one hand, these new movements are a "knock on the door of the church." Their objections to the state of affairs in the church should be heard and in many cases legitimate objections should cause us to repent of things we do or don't do that point up the incongruence of our lives and our failure to stay faithfully obedient to the gospel of Jesus Christ. But on the other hand, these movements pose a threat to the integrity of the church and of the gospel by focusing on a certain aspect of the truth at the expense of the whole truth and of the simplicity, integrity and balance of the gospel. Because of this, Christians need to carefully listen to and hear each other and support each other in the task of discipleship formation and the stimulation of theological and spiritual health in the church. But we should not be intimidated into the terrible choice that turns our eyes away from the one faithful center who is Jesus Christ himself.

New movements in the church challenge us to renewal and reformation. But when the challenge weakens our confidence in the total sufficiency of the gospel, then the situation is radically different and has nothing to do with renewal. It is instead the careful "set-up" of a Christian or group of Christians to make us so intimidated and broken in our discouragement that we are all the more easily drawn into the specialized doctrines of the new movement.

Therefore, in the face of all teaching, whether new and exciting or old and familiar, whether our own teaching or the teaching of others, we need to watch out for distortion, whether subtle or obvious. Paul gives some very helpful theological criteria and pastoral advice. He puts the matter into perspective with one clear and sharply worded sentence that will protect both the integrity of the Christian message and our own integrity: "We are the true circumcision who worship God in spirit, and glory in Christ Jesus, and put no confidence in the flesh." This is a central statement of fundamentals that will protect the Philippians from their legalistic "new-movement" detractors, and when we understand the statement in contemporary terms it will also clarify the kinds of false teaching that we face in our century.

Paul reminds the Philippians that the true and complete fulfillment of the Law and the prophets, and of the symbolic ritual that accompanied the Old Testament tradition, is found in Jesus Christ—and having said that he has said the most important thing there is to say. Since Christ as Lord is the only one who fulfills God's covenant with Abraham, we must watch out for any attempt to sneak any of the Old Testament rituals or signs of the covenant back into the gospel as if they had not already been fulfilled. Therefore, when we as human beings believe in God and trust in Jesus Christ, we have received in this one Lord all the richness of the Torah and the prophets as they have now converged in the fulfillment provided by God, his Son and our Messiah, Jesus Christ. Our task here and now is to listen to the Law and the prophets *through Jesus Christ.*

Note how this works out. We learn about the observance of the Sabbath day through Christ and the way he observed that day. We learn about "Thou shalt not kill" through our Lord Jesus Christ and by what he taught and what he did in the fulfillment of the intention of that great commandment. We trust in Christ and we are wise enough not to place any confidence in the special acts or procedures of any new legalism, whether we ourselves create it or others advocate it to us. (The term "flesh" is used by Paul to refer to acts we do in order to earn salvation.)

This one liberating sentence, "[We] worship God in spirit, and glory in Christ Jesus, and put no confidence in the flesh," should be written on our hearts and in our minds in order to keep us balanced and rightly centered on the Lord who is the true goal of all law and all ritual. Our acts of discipleship respond to the life in the Spirit that we have because of Christ's love, and therefore they respond to God's historical act in the life, death and victory of his Son, Jesus Christ, which was done in our favor.

Our most responsible action therefore is to "worship God in the Spirit" and to "glory in Christ Jesus." This is the only religious act that is needed from us and we should resist any attempts of devout religious people who now in effect reduce the adequacy of Christ by the addition of particular other acts that are placed alongside of, and thereby inevitably diminish, Christ's total adequacy. This is a clear case of subtraction by addition. Every time I add one more thing you need to do or have or learn in order to be really all that God wants you to be, I have by each added "enrichment" actually taken away from the sufficiency of the original starting point.

This is the problem of programs of piety that make the promise that there are mysteries to be learned beyond the basic relationship with the Lord of every mystery. These promises and the techniques they advocate must be carefully weighed to make certain that the additions to our mere Christian faith do not finally lead us toward the disastrous reductionism that takes away the best gift while promising better ones. Paul tells the Philippians, and through his letter to them he alerts all Christians, to watch out for any substitute for Jesus Christ.

The church itself and our involvement in its programs can become a substitute for Jesus Christ. The mission of the church can become a substitute for the living Lord of the mission. When this happens we begin to go adrift and to lose the true centeredness that keeps us Christians. We are on the way to detouring toward cults, and it all started by very small changes of focus, minute changes of heart.

Paul decides at this point to write autobiographically and personally. This personal style, which dominates the next few sentences in this letter, is another characteristic mark of Paul that is found in every letter. It seems to me that Paul is like the Old Testament prophet Jeremiah, whereas the apostle John is more like the prophet Isaiah. John and Isaiah do not write as much about their personal experiences and feelings. Paul and Jeremiah, on the other hand, tell much more about themselves. Paul allows his readers to know how he feels. In Paul's letters, as in the book of Jeremiah, we always find history lessons that show us the personal odyssey of the writer. What Paul now tells his friends at Philippi about himself is an emotionally charged, transparent, and even humorous narrative.

Paul tells us that from the perspective of first-century Judaism his mighty acts of devotion made him what amounted to a first-prize winner. He was circumcised, not as an adult, but on the eighth day of his life. This means that Paul was no last-minute convert to the tribe! He was a Jew, but better than that, he came from the best part of the Jewish nation. Furthermore, he belonged to the right religious group—not to the Sadducees, who compromised with the hated Roman conquerors, but to the Pharisees.

Pharisaism was a lay movement that began during the time after the Jews returned from the Babylonian exile under Ezra and Nehemiah. These separatists became a movement during the time of the Maccabeans. By the time of the first century the Pharisees were the most sincere and impressive believers among the people of Israel. As a young man Paul had studied under one of the great rabbis, Gamaliel, and he was thoroughly grounded in the Law and the prophets. He had more than an intellectual understanding of the Old Testament—he was a man of deep convictions. He persecuted the church mercilessly because he saw the followers of Christ as a threat to his deepest convictions and as a threat to the truth of God. Paul's fierce zeal, exemplified by his approval of the stoning of Stephen, was noted both by those within and by those outside the early church. He had concluded (and by the standards of Pharisaism correctly so) that he was righteous and complete.

Paul can never forget his harsh persecution of the early Christians. He had integrated his life around his understanding of God and God's truth as found in first-century Judaism, and his actions were congruent with his convictions. The anger was congruent and, as he later discovered, wrong, but it was consistent.

But Paul experienced a wrenching reversal that fundamentally changed his whole life. His focus and certainties were shattered by the blinding realization that he had been wrong, that his zeal and energy had been directed against the One who is the ultimate focus of the universe, Jesus Christ. Jesus Christ found Paul the terrorist. Paul was met by the grace of Jesus Christ the Lord, first on the road to Damascus, then in the small house of Ananias, and later in Tarsus, where Barnabas found him. Paul found a new integration and integrity through the shattering disintegration of what until then had been the focus of his life. It was not a simple matter. Paul spent several years in Arabia after his conversion experience (Gal 1:17), years he undoubtedly spent working through the implications of what had happened to him on the road to Damascus. His experience should help us remember that when someone comes to Christ, he or she is a new person, but we should allow time for God's Spirit to reintegrate that person's life. We should stand alongside that person in the (sometimes difficult) reintegration process, confident that God began a good work which he will bring to completion—not by our timetable but by his.

Paul creates a series of superlative contrasts, including one that contains what even by first-century social standards would be considered a crude literary expletive. These contrasts show the surpassing worth of Jesus Christ compared to any of the achievements and the fanatical consistency of his former life. None of these can compare with what Paul has found in the gospel of Jesus Christ, in whom this former legalist has found a righteousness "not . . . based on law, but that which is through faith in Christ." By comparison, all his former achievements he considers "refuse" *(skybalon)*. *Skybalon* means "dung, excrement, leavings, refuse." What he thought was the feast of God's approval was nothing but the garbage left over after the feast. Paul had been gnawing on chicken bones rather than on chicken, on the husks rather than the corn. In his legalistic achievement he had found no real food to nourish his life. He found true food in Christ. Note that Paul does not reject the Law as God's law, but he rejects the confidence that he had in himself because he kept the Law. Justification before God has come through *God's* fulfillment of the law in Christ. For Paul there can never again be "righteousness of my own based on law." Such a hope is empty pretense, it is "refuse."

We know from his letters to the Galatians and to the Romans that Paul teaches that the Law is the schoolmaster that brings us to Christ. It shows us what we should be like if we want to please God, and it shows us by contrast what we really are like. The Law is a holy mirror, but the Law cannot heal or cleanse the crises it reveals. The Law points to its Lord, but we wrongly understand the Law if we imagine that our devotion to its design is able to nourish and fulfill us. We need the Lord who is the author of the Law to fulfill the greatness revealed in the Law and to resolve the crises created by what the Law shows us about ourselves.

This is the discovery that Paul has made, and it is this discovery that encourages him to use the words "surpassing worth." It was not his own righteousness that made the decisive difference, it was faith. Faith for Paul means trusting in the faithfulness of God. The expression that Paul uses is literally "according to faith (in) Christ." The meaning is clear. Faith is seen as the *means*, not as the *source*, of justification.

When Paul thinks of faith he does not think of a brave act or an art form to be mastered as one might master some great and complicated skill. Faith responds to the evidence of God's self-evidence, and that is not so much a skill to be mastered as a relationship to be enjoyed. It is putting our weight on the faithfulness of God. This relationship now becomes the main focal point of the words that follow in this very moving autobiographical story of Paul's. Paul cannot speak only of the justification he has received in Christ. The Christian faith is not an impersonal ledger entry made in heaven—it is a relationship with Christ here and now, the relationship of an ordinary human being with the eternal Jesus Christ. We hear and read often about the Christian's "personal relationship with Jesus Christ." But what does it mean? It means that our existence, and the universe itself, rests, not on impersonal laws or on inexorable principles, but on a person. The gospel does not say merely that in the final analysis the universe is friendly toward us; it says that the God of the universe loves us. We sometimes feel like life is something very fragile and that we are in danger of stumbling into a spiral of chaos. The good news is that even if we fall, the "everlasting arms" that will catch us are underneath us (Deut 33:27). Our trust is not in theological principles, which all too often fail us when we are really in trouble, or in an intellectually coherent Christian world view, which can prove to be very brittle when the going gets tough. We trust in the One who upholds us even when we are too worried or depressed or excited to trust him. The ultimate foundation of our existence is personal.

Paul says that he wants "to know Christ and the power of his resurrection." He does not talk about some mystical experience of Christ, but about a congruence between his life and the life and person of Christ. It is an acceptance of and trusting in the ultimate validity of the truth of the "left-handed" power of God as exemplified in Jesus' life.

But knowing Christ involves, as Paul knows, more than those things we as human beings find naturally attractive and pleasant. It means that Jesus' way becomes our way, that his way to victory over death becomes our way—not because we have to earn salvation, or because we can in any way add to Christ's completed work. Rather, as Paul already made clear (Phil 2:3-11), Jesus' way of life, his self-emptying servanthood by which he became victorious, must be our way of life because it is the only way to true power and true life. Paul expresses his desire to be as totally identified with Christ as is possible and that includes Christ's suffering and death as well as his victory over death.

Christians will suffer for their faith. It may not be dramatic or spectacular. It may not be through persecution. More likely it is in the day-to-day learning to be a servant, to be obedient, and to be humble—not out of weakness but out of God-given strength. The curious thing is that those who are truly humble are usually not particularly aware of their humility, and the true heroes of the faith never seem to be aware of their heroism. Heroes are ordinary people who just stayed in a dangerous place a few minutes longer than all of the others—they were scared, but they stayed and so they became heroes. This is one of the remarkable facts about the brave saints throughout the ages. We have the privilege of getting a glimpse of those heroes of faith who wrote down the footnotes to their life stories or of those humble saints whom we know and whose consistently Christ-like lives shine in the midst of pedestrian surroundings. The heroes themselves, like Paul, are not really aware of the footnotes, and it is this matter-of-factness and lack of self-pity or self-consciousness that makes Paul's words so deeply impressive to us and gives us a clear example of what integrity is all about.

For Reflection:

1. "The non-Jewish believer does not need to become a Jew in order to know Christ's grace" (p. 124). Can you think of any requirements which are not part of the gospel of grace but which we as American Christians often impose on prospective believers or new converts?

2. What does the phrase "knowing Christ" mean to you personally—not only as a theological statement but especially as an experiential truth?

CHAPTER 14

PURITY
OF
HEART

Not that I have already obtained this or am already perfect; but I press on to make it my own, because Christ Jesus has made me his own. Brethren, I do not consider that I have made it my own; but one thing I do, forgetting what lies behind and straining forward to what lies ahead, I press on toward the goal for the prize of the upward call of God in Christ Jesus. Let those of us who are mature be thus minded; and if in anything you are otherwise minded, God will reveal that also to you. Only let us hold true to what we have attained. (PHIL 3:12-16)

Paul has been very specific and definite in his insistence that righteousness comes only from Christ and cannot be a "righteousness of our own." Since he has argued strongly against works righteousness, we might expect a peaceful doctrine of restful nonactivity. But Paul has nothing like that in mind. His experience of grace has produced more positive motivational energy than he had ever known in the self-righteous motivation of legalism.

In the next few verses Paul uses an image from the experience of the athlete committed to a race. There are two kinds of incentives that motivate team athletes. The one is the pressure on an athlete who is trying to win a place on the team. The other incentive is the pressure to excel that comes to a player because he or she is already on the team. Paul is describing that second motivation. We run the race, not in an attempt to somehow make the team, but because we are already on the team. The secret of Paul's motivation lies in his deep awareness of Jesus' unconditional acceptance. Paul presses on to make full identification with Christ his own because "Christ Jesus has made me his own." Paul's is not the motivation of fear, nor is it the motivation of guilt or of pride. It is the motivation of enthusiastic belonging. "I belong in this race, I was made for this event, this is my moment."

This awareness of being accepted gives Paul the freedom to focus on what is most important. He says that he does one thing: forgetting what lies behind and straining forward to what lies ahead, he presses toward the goal, the "final tape at the end of the runner's race." Every track and field competitor knows what Paul is talking about! In a race there is a forgetfulness of everything but the race itself. It is this forgetfulness and intensity of focus that Paul combines in these unforgettable sentences. Jesus' acceptance of the man, Paul, enables Paul to focus his personality—unlike the person who is uncertain of acceptance and who desperately runs in every direction in an attempt to find a place where he or she will feel accepted and secure.

Paul is able in this passage to be open and forthright about his own lack of perfection. He states twice in verse 12 that he has not yet "arrived": "Not that I have already obtained this or am already perfect." Paul's realism and his self-awareness do not immobilize or demoralize this runner because Paul has experienced the powerful grace and confidence of the Lord of the race toward Paul the contender. This is both a comfort and a warning. It is a comfort to those of us who feel inadequate as Christians. Paul had not yet arrived. We have not yet arrived. God does not expect us to have won the race, he expects us to run the race.

But it is also a warning for those of us who think that we have arrived spiritually. People who are spiritually self-satisfied are in danger of dropping out of the race and not reaching the goal at all. Later, in verse 15, Paul says, "Let those of us who are mature be thus minded." The word for mature, *teleios*, is from the same root as the word "perfect" in verse 12: "Not that I . . . am already perfect." This may be an intentional play on words on Paul's part: If you are mature, you know that you are not perfect; if you think you are perfect, you are not mature.

"Forgetting what lies behind and straining forward to what lies ahead." What is it Paul is advocating to us by these words? We often are unable to enjoy the present and to focus on what is truly important today because of guilt about our past and anxiety about our future. Guilt is the sense that we have done something wrong, whether it be a specific, all-too-well-remembered act or a vague sense of being guilty without being able to put our finger on exactly what it was we did wrong. We can feel guilty only about the past; we cannot feel guilty about the future. Anxiety, on the other hand, is what we feel about the future: uncertainty about what may happen or sometimes even the certainty that something terrible might possibly happen. Just as we cannot feel guilty about the future, we cannot be anxious about the past, although guilt and anxiety may be related. We may think that because we feel so guilty, there must be some kind of punishment waiting for us in the future. It is Paul's intention to face up to past, present and future.

There can be no whole perspective on life or the development of a philosophy of life that does not resolve our relationship with each of the three tenses of our life: past, present and future. Paul covers all three tenses in one sentence: "Forgetting what lies behind [past] and straining forward to what lies ahead [future], I press on [present]." He can make this statement with full conviction because the grace of God has resolved the guilt of his past and removed the anxiety about his future.

But we must read his statement in the light of what he has just said: "I am not yet perfect." The truth of God's grace is absolute, but our understanding and appropriation of that grace are not yet perfect. Growing in grace means learning more and more to live in the awareness that our guilt has been forgiven and that our future is secure in Christ—and that as a result we are truly free to live in the present. God will continue to do the work that he began in us when we came to Christ until we see him face to face. The good news is not that all our guilt feelings are erased in one stroke. The truly good news is that with God's help and the help of fellow Christians we can learn to face our guilt feelings and deal with our real or imagined guilt—knowing that, regardless of how and what we may feel, "there is now no condemnation" (Rom 8:1). For some of us, coming to grips with our guilt feelings and the causes of these feelings may be a long and difficult road. But God is at work in us!

This is why Paul now can "strain forward to what lies ahead"! Sprinters know that one instinctive habit that must be overcome is the temptation of a runner to look to the side to see where other competitors are in relationship to his or her own position on the track. When a runner turns slightly to look, there is a momentary loss of focus and rhythm that can be critical when a race is timed in fractions of seconds. On July 27, 1985, Steve Cram of Great Britain set a new world record in the World Mile Race at Oslo, Norway. He set a record at 3 minutes 46.31 seconds, breaking the 1981 record of Sebastian Coe. As I watched the spectacular Oslo race I was struck by the focused discipline of Cram as he held his lead position; only on one occasion by my calculation did he slightly turn to look for Coe and Gonzalez, who were following him.

It is this living metaphor that Paul has put into service to explain the way he understands the challenge of the Christian life. He avoids all "complacent, as against grateful, reflection."[1] Paul sees the Christian as living in the present, set free from the tyranny of the past and the future. But we must not misunderstand the apostle's word.

When Paul talks about "forgetting what lies behind," he is decidedly not antihistorical. He clearly remembers the past experiences of his life and they are an important part of who he is. In the same way Paul does not advocate to us a hollow kind of ignorance of the past with its legacies and lessons. A sense of history is important to each Christian. We cannot and should not forget our own personal past. God has worked in our lives in the past, and our memories of where we have been, which once filled us with guilt, can now begin to fill us with ever-growing gratitude for God's grace in our past. Denying our past and simply trying to push it out of our consciousness is dangerous, because it will continue to stalk us and will pounce on us when we least expect it. Facing the past and learning to understand it from the perspective of grace will lead us to a deeper appreciation of the good work that God has begun in us. Paul tells us to forget what lies behind in the sense that we must allow God's Spirit to break the hold our past and its guilt has over us so that we are free to live in the present and strive toward the future.

But the same is true also on a collective level: The church cannot be ahistorical. It cannot and must not forget its past. In too many evangelical churches we are tempted with the feeling that the Christian church begins in its Protestant experience with John Calvin or Martin Luther, or with D. L. Moody. The church began with Jesus Christ, and we can and should learn from the mistakes and triumphs, the understandings and misunderstandings of those who have gone before us through almost two millennia.

It is the Jesus Christ of history who as Living Lord is our companion by the Holy Spirit in the present, just as he is the one who resolved our past. Paul is not advocating for himself a present that is isolated from the past, a present in which we live day by day with new "spiritual" revelations of "present" truth. Cultic movements in the first century and since have preferred that sort of forgetfulness so that they might be able to create totally contemporary doctrines to fit contemporary situations. Paul's whole point is the very opposite. It is the Jesus Christ of history who has apprehended Paul in the past, who runs beside him in the present and who calls Paul toward the future. This same Jesus Christ is Lord of all three times of our existence—the past, the present and the future.

Paul now encourages his readers to think through the pattern of life which he has just described and which is the pattern of maturity: "Let those of us who are mature be thus minded." The word translated here as "be [thus] minded" is the Greek *phroneō*, which is a favorite word of Paul's (Rom 8:5, 7, 27; Col 3:2; and five times in Philippians: 1:7; 2:2; 2:5; 3:15; 4:10). The word has the meaning of "definite thinking, not of being in a mental state."[2] The word implies the hard work of thoroughly, carefully thinking something through. It is sometimes translated "to judge, think, form or hold an opinion" and "set one's mind on, be intent on." It is not merely thinking as an intellectual exercise, but thinking as an intellectual, moral and ethical effort.

The point is this. Paul calls on his readers to carefully think through for themselves the whole question of what constitutes the most healthy individual pattern of life. This passage is remarkable in that Paul on the one hand vigorously advocates a way of life that he has found for himself in his own journey with Christ and yet on the other hand avoids the oppressive paternalism that clutches at friends in order to control them. His double use of the word *phroneō* is decisive. Paul encourages the Christians at Philippi to evaluate carefully the apostle's counsel and to seek for themselves the guidance and confirmation from God's revelation of his will in Jesus Christ. All spiritual guidance should have this same built-in check. Every religious leader and teacher should encourage the learner to think through, on the basis of God's revelation of his will in the law and the gospel, every doctrine that is taught. All responsible theological statements should have the same accountability.

The Barmen Declaration, affirmed by the Confessing Church Movement in Germany in 1934, gives us a twentieth-century example of this principle. Listen to the opening sentences of Barmen: "If you find that we are speaking contrary to Scripture then do not listen to us! But if you find that we are taking our stand upon Scripture, then let no fear or temptation keep you from treading with us the path of faith and obedience."[3]

We should beware of religious leaders who do not encourage us as followers and learners to test all advice, all teaching, all exhortation by the standard of God's own revelation. This is the vital importance of the biblical test of all doctrine. Today, for example, there is a movement that claims that God wants all his children to be healthy and wealthy, that all a Christian has to do is claim health and prosperity, and God will give it. It is an attractive doctrine because it fits in so well with the American dream of success and because it simplifies reality by supposedly eliminating all that can create problems for us. But it flatly contradicts the many statements in the Bible about the place of suffering in the lives of the saints of both the Old and the New Testament. It certainly contradicts Paul's statement earlier in this chapter in Philippians, "that I may know him and the power of his resurrection, *and may share his sufferings.*" Claiming the power of the resurrection while rejecting the foundation of that power as shown in the life and death of Christ is in effect a form of claiming the world's right-handed power and rejecting God's left-handed power, which is the power of the resurrection.

Paul concludes this section by saying, "If in anything you are otherwise minded, God will reveal that also to you." It is one of the hallmarks of maturity and personal integrity that it allows others to have their own integrity. Paul does not tell us that if we are not in every respect like him, we are wrong. Rather, he trusts God to help us in our continued growth toward maturity and integrity. In a functional family, parents will allow their children to grow up, to mature in their own way and at their own rate, rather than forcing them into a rigid pattern of behavior that will retard the maturation process. The same is true in the church. When we deal with a new Christian, we can set an example, we can teach and we can listen, but we cannot force growth toward maturity. We must respect the integrity of the new Christian and allow him or her to grow in grace toward maturity and integrity according to God's timetable. We must be an example of maturity (which is much more difficult than being a religious drill sergeant) and thus work together with God to help the new Christian grow.

For Reflection:

1. What are the things you feel guilty about? What are the things you are anxious about? How might Paul counsel you concerning them?

2. "If in anything you are otherwise minded, God will reveal that also to you"—this is Paul's attitude toward those who are not yet mature. He has a radically different attitude toward those who are wrong (see, for example, Phil 3:2: "Look out for the dogs . . ."). How can we tell the difference between a believer who is immature and a believer who is wrong and needs correction?

CHAPTER 15

MODELS
OF
HOPE

Brethren, join in imitating me, and mark those who so live as you have an example in us. For many, of whom I have often told you and now tell you even with tears, live as enemies of the cross of Christ. Their end is destruction, their god is the belly, and they glory in their shame, with minds set on earthly things. But our commonwealth is in heaven, and from it we await a Savior, the Lord Jesus Christ, who will change our lowly body to be like his glorious body, by the power which enables him even to subject all things to himself.

Therefore, my brethren, whom I love and long for, my joy and crown, stand firm thus in the Lord, my beloved. (PHIL 3:17—4:1)

P aul now advises his readers to imitate the pattern of life they have observed in Paul. This advice does not contradict his earlier words of caution about blind and unthinking obedience to false teachers. Paul has made it clear that each believer is to think things through carefully, but now it is appropriate to remind them also that one of the proper ways we learn is by watching more experienced companions who are alongside us on our common journey. We learn by watching others.

Johann Sebastian Bach watched and listened carefully to the great organist-composer Dietrich Buxtehude. Bach's many trips to Buxtehude's church had a very definite influence upon the style and vitality of Bach's music and helped to shape the young Bach who would then go on to become an even greater genius than his mentor. Nevertheless, Bach needed the example and inspiration of this lesser genius. In the same way a skier learns to ski by watching an instructor skier and then learns through trial and error by imitating the teacher. We can study theology in isolation from others, but we cannot grow in grace by ourselves.

Paul then goes on to warn against those who are "enemies of the cross of Christ." Paul may have in mind here not only the legalists he challenged earlier, but also another movement which had its beginnings around the time Paul wrote this letter and which posed a serious threat to the integrity of the gospel: gnosticism (here in its early stages as pregnosticism). The pregnostic view taught that the body has no importance since we have a mystically spiritual relationship with Christ assured by secret knowledge. This would mean that the fully initiated believer is so totally spiritual that his or her personal actions are indifferent in the sight of God.[1] This view would lead to ethical and moral chaos.

If Paul is indeed on the attack against two kinds of error—rigid legalism on the one side and antinomian chaos on the other side—it is interesting that both attacks by Paul would find their place in the same sentences. This is because both legalism and gnosticism are opposed to the all-sufficiency and total lordship of Jesus Christ over all of life—body, soul, spirit. And in different ways we know that they each troubled the Christian churches of the first century. He then moves on to a grand design statement of the positive affirmation of the gospel.

The argument Paul gives against both legalism and gnosticism is that "our commonwealth is in heaven." Paul here uses the word *politeuma*, "commonwealth" (literally, "citizenship"), which is the noun form of the verb he used earlier, in 1:27: "Let your *manner of life* be worthy of the gospel of Christ." In chapter 1 Paul encouraged the Christians at Philippi to be real people in the real place where they live, so that their citizenship, that is their total community involvement and life, will show in concrete ways the gospel of Christ. Citizenship brings with it both privileges and responsibilities, and in chapter 1 Paul told the Philippians to take especially their social and political responsibilities as citizens seriously.

But Christians have a second set of privileges and responsibilities as citizens of heaven. The two citizenships are intertwined. If we fulfill our responsibilities as citizens of heaven (whose royal law is, "You shall love your neighbor as yourself" [Jas 2:8]), we will also be able to fulfill our responsibilities as citizens on this earth. On the other hand, if we are irresponsible citizens here and now, we cannot be responsible citizens of heaven! The practical everyday existence of Christian witness is possible because in a very profound sense our citizenship is in heaven. We live Christian lives in the real present with its concrete street addresses and political and social realities because we belong to a permanent citizenship that is God's gift to us here and now.

Some citizens of the United States live and work for a period of time in a foreign country. They have to live responsibly under the laws of that foreign country, just like its citizens. But at the same time they are subject to the laws of the United States. And no matter how wonderful the foreign country, the United States is home, it is the place where they ultimately belong and where they will go once their work in the foreign country is done.

But there is a difference. When we will finally fully claim our heavenly citizenship, Jesus Christ "will change our lowly body to be like his glorious body." The requirement for heavenly citizenship does not involve either circumcision or special gnostic secrets. Our bodies will be transformed, and this solid expectation is the best protection against religious leaders who insist upon either a religious rite like circumcision or a mystical religious breakthrough to make our bodies somehow acceptable to God. Such cosmetic religious acts are unnecessary since Christ will change our bodies as he chooses in accord with his grand design.

At the same time this expectation is the strongest argument against those who reject the body as if it were of no importance. The whole point of our hope of resurrection is that it is our concrete self that is beloved by Christ. We as real human beings really matter and that means our concrete self, our personality, our emotions, our distinctive characteristics—the total mixture of who we are is beloved by Jesus Christ and it is the particular "who we are" that has a destiny in the fulfilled commonwealth. Therefore we do not take ourselves lightly just as we do not worship ourselves.

Integrity involves both of these citizenships. We cannot have integrity in our everyday affairs if we are not willing to take seriously our responsibilities as citizens of heaven. And we cannot possibly have integrity as citizens of heaven if we neglect the interpersonal, social and political responsibilities as citizens here on earth.

Paul concludes this section with an appeal to "stand firm in the Lord." And he makes that appeal a very personal one. He asks the Philippians to stand firm because he cares very deeply for them: "My brethren, whom I love and long for, my joy and crown, . . . my beloved." You cannot get more personal than that. The word *stefanos*, "crown," is the Greek word for a crown of victory, such as the wreath that would be worn by a returning warrior or a champion athlete. It should not be confused with the word *diadēma*, which is the Greek word for the crown worn by a king. Paul does not have notions of kingly reign for himself, but he does have the vision of the wreath of acknowledgment for the race run and he tells the Philippians that they have been for him already that good wreath. In effect he tells them, "You're my celebration wreath, my gold medal."

After talking about our citizenship in heaven, Paul exhorts the Philippians to "stand firm." But we should note that when Paul talked about our earthly citizenship (our "manner of life") in 1:27, he similarly follows it up with the exhortation to "stand firm." Our way of life in both realms must be consistent. We must live in both realms with integrity—an integrity rooted in the sure knowledge that Jesus Christ himself is the only lasting foundation upon whom we may build, and that we are able to build on that sure foundation because we are accepted unconditionally by God.

For Reflection:

1. In what areas do you fall short as a citizen of heaven? In what areas do you measure up?

2. In what areas do you fall short as a citizen of this earth? In what ways do you measure up?

3. Is there any relationship between the two lists?

CHAPTER 16

THE GOSPEL
FOR
PEOPLE IN STRESS

I entreat Euodia and I entreat Syntyche to agree in the Lord. And I ask you also, true yokefellow, help these women, for they have labored side by side with me in the gospel together with Clement and the rest of my fellow workers, whose names are in the book of life. (PHIL 4:2-3)

W ho are Euodia, Syntyche and Clement? The first two names are common first-century names and we know nothing more about them than what we have in this narrative. Clement is also a common first-century name, but the early church fathers Origen and Eusebius were convinced that this Clement is the man who later became a bishop in Rome and wrote the letter of Clement to the Corinthians

(A.D. 110-120). Some interpreters of Philippians have constructed an elaborate interpretive scheme to explain these names, proposing that the two female names symbolize two parties or factions within the church, "the Jewish Christians and the Gentile Christians." Such an interpretive model is totally artificial and in the end much less helpful than the simpler, literary approach. The most valuable interpretive model to follow in all Old and New Testament studies is the hermeneutical rule, "lean is better than luxurious." The simplest and most obvious meanings of words and names should be the primary method of interpretation.

This means that, in the absence of other information about them, we must assume that what we have here is a direct reference by Paul to three actual people who are members of the fellowship at Philippi. It is not clear from the paragraph whether the argument only involves Euodia and Syntyche, while Clement is one of the yokefellows who is to assist in their reconciliation, or whether Clement himself is also in some way a party to the dispute and for that reason is named by Paul.

What I think is a point of great importance is that Paul has not become so involved in the gossip and stories of conflict that he is willing to make the connections clear to us. The members of the church at Philippi who received this letter knew the answers to the questions we have about the dispute. But from Paul we will learn no gossip about particulars. Instead, what we have in these few simple sentences of the apostle is the example of a remarkably sensitive pastor-counselor who manages to become involved in a way that preserves the integrity of all parties and preserves the high reputation of each person, while at the same time realistically facing up to the fact of an interpersonal crisis in the church community.

The wise mixture of pastoral elements in these few lines from

Paul is very helpful for those of us who must face similar conflict situations in a fellowship. Notice what Paul says and what he does not say. He does not take sides in the dispute. He does not from a distance try to produce a narrative of the causes of the crisis. He does not give the church detailed disciplinary instructions. He does not threaten or scold either the persons involved or the church. Yet at the same time he does not gloss over the crisis in a vague or indirect way.

Notice what he does say. He names the persons in a forthright way. He admits to a crisis of disagreement in the church. He calls on the parties involved to agree in the Lord. While acknowledging that there are points of view or convictions or behavior patterns in which they do not stand together, he encourages them to meet where they do stand together—their common bond in the lordship of Christ. The advice is profoundly theological. Paul points to the fact that because of Jesus Christ we as Christians are not left alone to figure out and to solve our interpersonal relationships as if our direct relationship with other fallible and imperfect human beings were all we have. Dietrich Bonhoeffer made the profound observation that, because of Christ the Savior Lord and his radical intervention, we now have *mediated* relationships with each other in the family of faith as well as *mediated* relationships toward those outside faith and indeed toward the whole created order. "Christ stands between us and God, and for that very reason he stands between us and all other men and things."[1]

The difference for us within the commonwealth of faith is that we, like Euodia and Syntyche and Clement, know of the lordship of Christ, so that like these sisters and this brother we may come together and stand together in Christ. The church has known differences of opinion and disagreements for almost two thousand years. The problem is not that these disagreements exist, but that so frequently relatively insignificant points of disagreement are infused with a false sense of importance. They overshadow and make us lose sight of the one thing that *is* of ultimate importance: Jesus Christ and his reign. This is the bedrock of our relationship with God and with each other. And it is only when we recognize this fundamental primary agreement in Christ that we are able to frankly and creatively work on the resolution of the secondary points of disagreement.

Paul and Peter demonstrated to the church this approach toward interpersonal and doctrinal disagreements in their encounter at Antioch and its subsequent resolution (see Galatians 2 and Acts 15). Peter and Paul found their most basic common footing in the all-sufficiency of Christ, and from this shared loyalty and basic beginning place they were able to work toward theological clarity. And each was able to preserve his integrity throughout the whole experience of their disagreement.

Paul goes on to ask the "yokefellow" to help. Yokefellow is the word *syzygos*, which is a word that only appears in this sentence in the New Testament. It means "comrade," and combined with the word *gnēsios* should be translated "true, genuine comrade." The singular noun is used, which may indicate that Paul is instructing one particular individual in the church, or it may be a rhetorical singular that refers to the church fellowship as a whole as Paul's "true comrade." Although it seems to me that Paul intends the singular to refer to the church as a whole, either way simple and straightforward. The church (or a ual in the church) is challenged to find a way to . Notice that Paul leaves the details and specific e church. Paul merely indicates the direction in ld go. The means by which they provide help is committed to their judgment; the goal is to "help" lift together these disciples in stress.

I am impressed by Paul's confidence in the ability of amateurs to be of real help. We, the church members who are to "help" one another in times of stress, are ordinary people ourselves. When our motives are clearly set toward encouragement and wholeness, then the results can be encouraging and unifying. I know from personal experience that it works. We who live in an age of experts need to remember and be reminded that *people are helped by people*. Paul, the expert, does not prescribe a cure for the argument at Philippi but instead turns it over to the family at Philippi. He gives them guidelines and encouragement, but the message is crystal clear: *They* must do the helping and *they* must find the help that best fits the situation.

Finally, the apostle reminds the helper or helpers that they must not forget that Euodia, Syntyche and Clement worked side by side with Paul in the service of the gospel. In spite of their disagreement, they are Paul's colleagues and he wants the church to remember that and to show them respect even as they offer help. This is wise counsel because one of the most dangerous side effects of the "helping" professions is that professional or volunteer helpers sometimes fail to respect the people who are under their care. They see themselves as reaching down to those in need of their help instead of reaching out to a fellow human being. For example, patients in a hospital are so completely surrounded by reminders of their helplessness and their need to be helped that they often lose their dignity as human beings. At the same time the hospital staff is so continuously surrounded by helplessness and dependency (and lack of adequate staffing) that they begin to treat patients as cases to be cured rather tha' people who are suffering.

Paul wisely advocates a twofold strategy for helping those in need without losing respect for them. First, the church must remember that these persons in crisis are colleagues of the apostle; the argument between them has not put into jeopardy their highly treasured relationship with Paul. Second, Paul reminds the church that the names of Euodia, Syntyche and Clement are written here and now in the Book of Life. We know from references to this expression in other places in the Old and New Testaments (Is 4:3; Lk 10:20; Rev 3:5; etc.) that this inscription refers to the Lord's knowledge of these two women and Clement and of God's present and eternal acceptance of them.

Paul gives us an example in all of this of how to deal with conflict in the church. First, by his refusal to discuss the specific issue and by writing only about the people involved, he shows that people must always take precedence over disagreements. It is very easy when we get involved in a disagreement to develop tunnel vision and see those who disagree with us no longer as people but as opponents. We see them only in terms of our disagreement. We and the church become polarized over an issue because of this narrow vision.

Paul, on the other hand, focuses on the larger picture that sees these two women, not as opponents but as fellow workers in the past and fellow children of God in the present. He reminds the church of his own respect for Euodia and Syntyche because of the help and support they have given him. But most importantly, he reminds them of the ultimate truth about these two women: God loves them and accepts them. Compared to this eternal truth, any present disagreement is transitory and insignificant.

Later in this chapter (v. 8) Paul states the very same principle in more general terms: "Whatever is true, whatever is honorable, whatever is just, whatever is pure, whatever is lovely, whatever is gracious, if there is any excellence, if there is anything worthy of praise, think about these things." How many church conflicts could be forestalled or minimized if we applied this when we think and talk about other people—especially the ones we don't get along with too well. It would help us maintain our own integrity and protect the integrity of others.

For Reflection:

1. In the past, have you experienced disunity in your church or in another church you were associated with? What happened? Reread this chapter in light of that situation. What could have been done to avoid or resolve the conflict?

2. What are areas of potential disunity in your church right now? Why? What are possible preventive measures? How can you have an encouraging effect on your church? What are some ways your church can become an encouraging fellowship?

CHAPTER 17

FOCUSED INTEGRITY

Rejoice in the Lord always; again I will say, Rejoice. Let all men know your forbearance. The Lord is at hand. Have no anxiety about anything, but in everything by prayer and supplication with thanksgiving let your requests be made known to God. And the peace of God, which passes all understanding, will keep your hearts and your minds in Christ Jesus.

Finally, brethren, whatever is true, whatever is honorable, whatever is just, whatever is pure, whatever is lovely, whatever is gracious, if there is any excellence, if there is anything worthy of praise, think about these things. What you have learned and received and heard and seen in me, do; and the God of peace will be with you. (PHIL 4:4-9)

The church in Philippi has many things to be worried or preoccupied about. Epaphroditus has hardly proved to be a very durable missionary helper for the beloved Paul; he became ill in a short time and found it necessary to return home. Paul himself is in grave danger, and though Paul makes a brave, optimistic statement about his hopes to return to Philippi, the people in Philippi will know after the report from Epaphroditus that Paul's release from prison is very unlikely. The church struggles with the controversy over the difficult issue of legalism from the Jewish side of the fellowship and perhaps also with the early beginnings of gnostic spiritualization from the Greek side of the fellowship. And then there is the argument between prominent church leaders: Euodia and Syntyche, and possibly Clement as well.

Each of these reasons is cause for alarm, embarrassment, and discouragement because each of these in a different way calls into question the durability of the gospel and of the gospel's people to withstand the intensity of the pressures of the first-century world with its confusion, decadence and needs. Paul's shout of joyous confidence from Nero's prison, "Rejoice in the Lord always; again I will say, Rejoice," stands at the forefront of all defiant shouts of faith from out of the depths. I especially like the comment of Karl Barth on this sentence: " 'Joy' in Philippians is a defiant 'nevertheless!' which Paul sets like a full stop against the Philippians' anxiety."[1] The exuberance of Paul's great sentence has been one of the wonderful gifts to Christians of all time. "Rejoice in the Lord always; again I will say, Rejoice."

This is different from the glib phrase people often use, "Cheer up, things could be worse." Paul does more than to tell the Philippians (and us) to rejoice. He backs up his exhortation with a number of statements that at first glance appear to be unrelated.

But we should always assume that there is an inner coherence in what Paul says. One statement leads to another, and there is always a connection, even if it is not immediately apparent. Paul's train of thought is not always linear, that is, he does not always write in strictly logical sequences in which each statement follows obviously from the preceding one. Rather, he often presents a cluster of statements that, taken together, paint a picture. This is what he does here. In the verses that follow his exhortation to "rejoice always" he mentions a number of things that will make this possible.

First he says, "Let all men know your forbearance." The word for forbearance, *epieikēs*, means "yielding, gentle, kind." The word carries the connotations of openness, relaxation, moderation, gentleness. It is the same word that is used in James 3:17: "But the wisdom from above is first pure, then peaceable, *gentle*, open to reason, full of mercy and good fruits." Today we might use the word "mellowness." There is a connection between the ability to rejoice in the Lord and one's attitudes toward others. Paul is urging his friends to be cool.

We should also note that right before his exhortation to "rejoice in the Lord always" Paul was talking about divisions and disagreements in the church at Philippi. He seems to imply that our attitude toward others, even when we disagree with them, has a direct bearing on our ability to rejoice in the Lord. A negative attitude toward others and an unwillingness to treat them with gentleness will keep us focused on the negatives and captive to our own resentments and hurts. It will not allow us to be free to rejoice in the Lord, to enjoy the freedom we have in him. Paul here models a fascinating mixture of the enthusiastic shouts of joy and the inner and interpersonal quality of moderateness, mellowness. Often an attitude of harshness toward others is motivated by guilt: we see in others the same weaknesses and short-comings we see in ourselves but are unwilling to admit to. For example, it is no accident that those who continuously talk about the evils of sex, of pride, or of selfishness often have serious problems in these ethical areas themselves.

But if unresolved guilt about the past and in the present is an enemy of mellowness and gentleness, so is anxiety about the future. And thus Paul follows his exhortation to exhibit a yielding spirit and mellowness with what may seem to be an unrelated statement but is not: "The Lord is at hand." We cannot be truly mellow and we are unable to truly rejoice if we are anxious about the future. But the future is in the hands of God! The Lord is near. He resolves history at its ending just as he stands at history's beginning and just as he is history's radical center. Jesus Christ is the "Enormous Exception" (G. K. Chesterton) who makes the real difference. This is the deep resource for freedom from panic or desperation that Paul describes by this remarkable word choice *epieikēs*. The Christian is open toward life in the present because Christ reigns.

And this is precisely what Paul says next: "Have no anxiety about anything." The word translated "anxiety" *(merimnaō)* means "anxious, harassing care."[2] It is the word Peter uses in his famous sentence in 1 Peter 5:7: "Cast all your anxieties on him, for he cares about you." It is also the word used by Jesus in the Sermon on the Mount: "Therefore do not be anxious about tomorrow" (Mt 6:34).

Paul now encourages the Christians at Philippi to challenge the real harassment of continuous and low-grade fear by bringing their whole selves with the requests that they have in their hearts and minds directly to the Lord. Paul draws two words together to explain the act of prayer by which we bring our requests to the Lord. *Proseuchomai* is the word translated by the English word "pray" in the New Testament. Because of the prefix *pros* it should more precisely be translated "pray toward." The *pros* gives a vital clue to the reader that biblical prayer is focused primarily on or toward the One to whom we pray, rather than upon the act of prayer or the practice of prayer as a religious act of the believer.

The word *deēsis* is the word translated "petition," and it means the specific request made to God. Prayer in the Bible is the specific and definite thinking in which we think things through before God. Paul encourages exactly this kind of thoughtful prayer by his use of this word. We are invited by our friend Jesus Christ, who showed us how to pray in the Lord's prayer, to bring the requests and real concerns of our daily lives, including our need for bread, to the Father in prayer. Now Paul reminds the Philippians of that generous invitation. The third key word in Paul's invitation to prayer is the word "thanksgiving." We must focus, not only on what we need, but also on what the Father has given us—which should fill us with thanksgiving and with the confidence that God hears our prayer.

Paul has backed up his exhortation to rejoice with three specifics, each dealing with a different relationship: mellowness toward others, a lack of anxiety toward the world and the future because the Lord is near, and a prayerful relationship with God. Now he adds a fourth, which is the result of the first three and concerns us as individuals and also collectively as the church: "And the peace of God, which passes all understanding, will keep your hearts and your minds in Christ Jesus." This is the peace that belongs to God and is his alone to grant. As we have seen earlier, "peace" in the Old Testament Hebrew is the word *šhālôm*, which is a very rich word that contains the sense of wholeness and health. Paul here writes in Greek, but the rich and ancient Hebrew word certainly stands behind this first-century expression. This peace far exceeds, is far above, every thought and will guard our lives. ("Guard" is a better word than the RSV "keep." The word *phroureō* means to "guard" or "garrison," and the noun form of this word is the word for "fort" or "fortress." What a powerful peace!) Paul informs us that God's peace is able to guard our hearts and our minds from the pressures that cause the harassment and fear.

For many centuries these words of Paul were treasured for their poetic beauty but hardly for their realism. But everything changes! The massive fortresses of ancient and medieval history have been replaced in Western history by weapons and strategies of war. Because of the technological achievements in weapon invention, we who live in the nuclear generation are now able to really understand the profound inner truth and realism of Paul's affirmation that peace is a fortress.

If two people are standing across the room from each other and the floor is covered with gasoline, the best protection for each person is to talk with the other and to keep away from matches. The extensive fire power of modern weaponry has produced just this sort of mutual restraint between the atomic-arsenal nations, who now realize that the world's surest fortress for each country on the globe is peaceful arms-reduction negotiations between nations that will hopefully lead to peace in this nuclear, gasoline-on-the-floor world.

But Paul has in mind the even more profound peace that comes from the love of Jesus Christ at work in the hearts and minds of people. This sentence directs our eyes toward the mystery of the gospel of Jesus Christ that is able to create new beginnings and is able to heal brokenness. When warfare is raging in a human life, the result of this inner conflict is that we cause harm to the neighbor unfortunate enough to be nearby. There can be no realistic peace in human life, nor between human beings, unless this most basic of all warfare is slowed down and finally resolved.

But our own experiences with the harsh realities of human sin and our own skill at doing harm have made us pessimistic about real solutions. Paul fully understands our difficulty in expecting any lasting resolutions of this long-term crisis, and that is why he announces the power of the peace that comes from Jesus Christ as the peace that surpasses our best estimates or expectations.

But Paul adds one more facet to the picture he has painted in these verses. He tells us that we need to focus our thinking: "Think about these things." The verb *logizomai* means "to think carefully and thoughtfully." We cannot rejoice, be gentle, look forward to the Lord's return, and pray if we are preoccupied by the evil and problems around us. Paul tells us not to think positive thoughts (which can be very self-centered and are often not much more than wishful thinking), but to focus on whatever is just, pure, lovely, gracious, excellent and worthy of praise.

Paul's selection of the eight virtues in this sentence should not be seen as Paul's attempt at a complete list of all possible virtues but, rather, as examples to stir the imagination and awareness of the Christians. Paul calls upon those who have their minds in Christ to now think through and meditate upon those values that are true, honorable, just, pure, lovely, gracious, excellent, worthy of praise—but not merely to make us feel better or as an exercise in positive thinking. Paul immediately follows his exhortation to think about that which is good by the command to *do*. There is an intimate connection between what we think and what we do. That which fills our minds will sooner or later translate into action. If all we read are novels that endorse ethical relativism, we will lose our sensitivity to the difference between right and wrong actions. If all we watch are movies that celebrate violence, we will become insensitive to the evil of violence.

The word for "do" in verse 9 is *prassō*, from which we derive our words "practice" and "praxis." The Christian faith for Paul is thoughtful because it is grounded in Jesus Christ who is the truth, and it is practical because our thoughtful meditation on that which is good will, and must, express itself in everyday life.

This paragraph is reminiscent of the Old Testament book of Proverbs. Paul adopts the wisdom approach of the Jewish proverb in order to alert his readers to virtues which are all directly related to integrity. The Hebrew word that is translated "wisdom" in the Old Testament is the word that means "skill." As we read the wisdom texts of the Old Testament, such as the book of Proverbs and the Psalms, we discover in that literature the rich Jewish tradition of the teaching of ethical, moral and spiritual skills to young men and women so that they will know how to live as God intended them to live. Paul decides to play that ancient role with the Philippian Christians, not to reintroduce legalism, but instead to help them grow in the gospel. Paul's point is that we as growing Christians need to examine values that make up the range of possible behavior patterns, to choose the substantial patterns that we have observed in the lives of people like Paul himself, and then to put into practice what we know to be true and healthy.

Paul has put his finger on a very important truth about spiritual-ethical growth. Growing as a Christian in a healthy way requires from the Christian thousands of day-by-day decisions about values. Each of these decisions involves possibilities that we must evaluate for ourselves, and we must then follow up our choices with "praxis" concreteness. We, and only we, are able to choose what behaviors will become our own. But inevitably those day-to-day choices make up the portrait of who I really am. The large, grand goals, such as peace and justice, are easy to embrace and admire with beautiful rhetoric in the abstract. But all too often we are like the Peanuts character Linus, who said, "I love mankind, it's people I can't stand." The large, grand goals become reality in a human life on the basis of the day-to-day, small-scale choices that we make in supermarkets, on the freeway, in crowded work stations, at home, and in a thousand other forks in the road where we made the real choices that either express or diminish the grand goals that have won our respect.

For this reason Paul calls out to the Christians at Philippi to choose the ways that honor the substantial values. Paul is encouraging us to make a habit of the virtues we treasure so that they become a regular part of each day. He wants us to practice the virtues we believe in just as we practice an athletic skill in order to make that skill a regular and natural part of our daily lives.

I know from experience that Paul is giving the right advice to these friends of his. I know that honesty needs to be the practical everyday pattern in my life, and there are countless opportunities to practice honesty in the many small details of my ordinary interpersonal encounters. Great moments for great acts of sacrificial love rarely announce themselves to us with adequate lead time. Instead, we stumble into the most important moments in odd places and seemingly insignificant situations, so that it is only later that we understand what really happened.

Courage is like that. Brave people who we honor with awards for public courage are usually ordinary people who stayed close to danger just a few seconds longer than everyone else, and while they stayed they thought up something concrete to do that turned out to be a courageous act at a time of intense stress. The brave man or woman was just as frightened as everyone else, but something made those added seconds possible. In most instances it was their pattern of living and their habits of doing things that played the big part. We gradually become brave just as we gradually learn how to really communicate with our children or our parents. Paul wants the kind of Christians at Philippi who, like a weight lifter working out every day with weights, daily practice their virtues. It means putting them into practice when no one is watching.

Paul began by exhorting the Philippians to rejoice and showed them practical ways to make it possible for them to do so. The result will be that "the peace of God . . . will keep your hearts and your minds in Christ Jesus." Then he told them to focus their minds on whatever is truly worth focusing on and to follow Paul's example. And the result will be that "the God of peace will be with you." Integrity of perspective, which is what Paul has been talking about in this section, enables us to rejoice and to experience the peace of God, and the giver of that peace, the God of peace.

For Reflection:

1. In Philippians 4:6 Paul makes a statement that is almost ludicrous when we hear it in the context of our society: "Have no anxiety about anything." Spend some time (whether ten minutes or ten weeks!) meditating on this statement in the larger context of 4:4-9 (ignore the break that is inserted between verses 7 and 8 in the RSV!).

2. Is Philippians 4:8 pie-in-the-sky-head-in-the-sand theology?

How does it differ from a naive optimism and from a refusal to live in the world? In a society that bombards us with written and spoken messages and information, how can we begin to implement Paul's exhortation?

CHAPTER 18

THE GENEROSITY
OF
LOVE

I rejoice in the Lord greatly that now at length you have revived your concern for me; you were indeed concerned for me, but you had no opportunity. Not that I complain of want; for I have learned, in whatever state I am, to be content. I know how to be abased, and I know how to abound; in any and all circumstances I have learned the secret of facing plenty and hunger, abundance and want. I can do all things in him who strengthens me. Yet it was kind of you to share my trouble. And you Philippians yourselves know that in the beginning of the gospel, when I left Macedonia, no church entered into partnership with me in giving and receiving except you only; for even in Thessalonica you sent me help once and again. Not that I seek the gift; but I seek the fruit which increases to your credit. I have received full payment, and more; I am filled, having received from Epaphroditus the gifts you sent,

a fragrant offering, a sacrifice acceptable and pleasing to God. And my God
will supply every need of yours according to his riches in glory in Christ Jesus.
To our God and Father be glory for ever and ever. Amen.

Greet every saint in Christ Jesus. The brethren who are with me greet you.
All the saints greet you, especially those of Caesar's household. The grace of
the Lord Jesus Christ be with your spirit. (PHIL 4:10-23)

P aul ends the letter to the Philippians with a personal note of gratitude. But, as is typical of Paul's writings, even something as simple as saying thank you turns into a long paragraph with profound moments of spiritual and practical insight. Paul thanks his good friends at Philippi for their persist-ent search for him so that they could extend their practical help to him. Perhaps they lost track of the apostle during Paul's trial at Jerusalem and during his two years at Caesarea (Acts 24—26) and certainly during the long ship journey to Rome (Acts 27). But they finally discovered his whereabouts in Rome, and they have sent their own young missionary to help Paul.

As we have seen, Roman prisons of the first century were dangerous places, and if a prisoner did not have friends outside of the prison to help with food supplies and other needs the prisoner would not have regular food and provision for his needs. Nevertheless Paul is not preoccupied with his situation and he wants the Philippians to know that he is not discouraged. And in this context Paul shares with them one of his most un-forgettable sentences of faith.

Paul has learned during his journey of faith the secret of facing the sharp contrasts of fortune and misfortune that have been a part of his life as an ambassador of Jesus Christ. The word Paul uses for "I have learned" is *myeō*, which can also mean "to be initiated into a secret." What is Paul's secret? What has enabled

Paul to take life in stride? Paul's answer is clear. It is his living day to day in relationship with Jesus Christ who empowers him along the way. Dietrich Bonhoeffer made the same discovery in his twentieth-century prison. "I believe God will give us all the power we need to resist in all time of distress. But he never gives it in advance lest we should rely upon ourselves and not on him alone."[1] What a secret! So basic and so available to all who have simple faith in Jesus Christ. The spiritualistic and legalistic elites will be very disappointed by the great apostle's words, but Paul has in this realistic confessional statement set generations of Christians free from cultic experts in religious secrets. They are unneeded because the living relationship of a believer with Jesus Christ is the only secret we need.

Abounding prosperity and devastating hardship—Paul has experienced each, and he wants his friends to know that he has been able to take each in stride because of the companionship of Jesus Christ. One of the hallmarks of Christian integrity and personal integration is that circumstances lose their overwhelming power over us. Our self-image and sense of security no longer are tied to the things that happen to us. Events are important, but for Paul something is more important and he has learned it by experience.

Paul's secret lies in the realization that both abundance and abasement are relative and transitory. Paul does not make either the one or the other more important or less important than it is. Abundance and want are simple. These are things that happen, and Paul has learned the secret of taking each in stride. The key is that he lets them happen without an overinterpretation of their long-term significance because Jesus Christ already has won that long-term significance. I believe that this is at the heart of the secret.

Most people who are confused and harmed by abundance or loss are the ones who confer permanence on either. But the fact is that at the heart of the existence of each of us is something of far greater durability and importance. It is Jesus Christ, the companion of our way, who outlasts both extremes as well as any degree of abundance and abasement in between— they are merely way stations on our journey. Paul can enjoy a steak and lobster without any problem at all, and he accepts the shipwreck too. He is not too impressed by extravagance, which is nice once in a while, or by intense abuse, which is hard to take but, like abundance, is not the last word. That is Paul's secret.

Paul admits that he needs the strengthening of Jesus Christ in order to handle both success and hardship. It is a wonderful breakthrough for us when we really see his point. We need strength to handle the many wide swings of fortune, whether they are positive or negative. We, in and of ourselves, do not have the resources to keep a clear perspective when these swings take place because each has a temptation hidden within it. On the one side there is the temptation to pride and on the other side there is the temptation to despair. Paul knows his own limitations and he does not portray himself in triumphant terms. He knows himself too well to believe in any secret of power within himself. Paul can take things in stride because of the One who strides alongside him, and he has found his true pace by walking with the Lord in the places where the journey takes him, where paths are hard or where the lines fall in pleasant places. The secret is the focal point of his life, the center around which his life is integrated. As he focuses his vision on God and his love as seen in Jesus Christ, all other things automatically are relegated to the realm of peripheral vision. The other things are still there, and we are still aware of them, but their sharp contours are softened and they do not occupy the center of our awareness.

Now Paul continues his final words of thanks to the Philippians by expressing his gratitude to them for "sharing his trouble." This was not the first expression of support Paul had received from the church in Philippi. Ever since Paul's first visit to Philippi with Silas, Luke and Timothy, they as a fellowship had been his most supportive church, and "even in Thessalonica you sent me help once and again." Immediately after his first visit to Philippi Paul went to Thessalonica, which was a much wealthier city than Philippi, and thus the generosity of the Philippian church toward Paul was expressed from the very beginning of their relationship with Paul.

Paul makes it clear that their gifts over the years have a larger significance than their most obvious intention of assistance from one church fellowship to a person in Rome whom they considered a part of their church. There are no hints whatsoever that the Philippians have not given enough or should send more. On the contrary, Paul speaks of being "filled" by their gifts. Their gifts have an importance beyond their helpfulness to him because they are also in themselves creative. The word he uses is "fruitful." In other words, they have a way of growing beyond their own boundaries. How can this happen? I think I know from experiences of my own life, and one family incident particularly stands out in my memory.

In 1976 our family took a major trip in connection with a summer study leave I had received from our church. Just a few days before we were to leave on this trip a neighbor of ours who was a member of our church visited my wife, Shirley, and gave her a check for $100, telling her that we were to use this money any way we wanted to on our trip. We were totally surprised by this gift, so we bought $100 in traveler's checks to be used in accordance with this neighbor's generous suggestion. It would be for our trip "the Spanne money," the unexpected gift of George and Louise Spanne.

Our first stop was Kyoto, Japan, where we met up with a Japanese family who were friends of other members of our church in Berkeley. This delightful family went with our family to visit the zoo and several gardens in that old capital city of Japan. When we came back to the hotel Shirley and I invited these new friends to have tea with us in the lobby of the hotel. Each of us had a cup of tea, and their two children and our three children had soft drinks. I received my first severe jolt about Japanese restaurant costs when the bill for this tea (no cakes or even crackers) came to $75. I was shocked, and later that evening we as a family made plans to move on from Japan as soon as possible just to stay solvent. But then a thought occurred to me that made us all feel much better. I pointed out to our traveling band that we had the $100 extra money from the Spannes, which covered the unexpected restaurant bill—with $25 to spare.

Later on our trip other occasions occurred that were similar. In the Philippines we found that we really wanted to give some gifts that were beyond our budget plans, but we remembered that there was still $25 of the Spanne money left—in fact more, because in Kyoto we would have had to use our regular money for that tea had we not had the extra $100. So we felt much better with the added supply of Spanne money. By now we all called this harvest of funds the Spanne money. Do you know that those funds never seem to run out? Members of our family would cheerfully remind me, and they still do some fourteen years later, at moments when we really want to make an important expenditure—"But Dad, we always have the Spanne money." I couldn't bring myself to challenge the endlessness of their figuring because I felt something good was happening to them. They were themselves learning how to be generous with money, and they were learning that a gift given in love always multiplies and bears its own kind of fruit far beyond our expectations so that we need some very modern math to figure it out.

This is what I believe Paul is talking about when he tells the Philippians that their kindness toward him is having a multiplying effect. Paul puts their gifts in a much broader perspective by reminding them that their gifts are pleasing to God and that they constitute a fruit, a fragrant offering, a sacrifice that honors God who is the source of all gifts. God does not accept men's and women's sacrifices to atone for human sins, but God accepts the gifts of our concern and involvement as a sacrifice of gratitude, and that sacrifice pleases him.

Paul teaches the Philippians a new understanding of sacrifice. It is the love that overflows as a *result* of our redeemed life in Christ that now becomes the New Covenant fulfillment of the ancient religious rites of sacrifice, which had sought by ritual to signal the establishment of that right relationship with God.

Religious rituals, especially the rituals of various kinds of sacrifice, have made up a large part of the practice of religion throughout human history, and many of these rituals of sacrifice have been grim and brutal acts that have stained the history of every religion with horror and confusion. What Paul has done is to call into question for the Philippians and for us every sacrificial procedure and ritual that has preoccupied religious men and women. We want to sacrifice things and animals and even people because we feel our helplessness and alienation. It is an attempt on our part to find God, and Paul has challenged the essential logic that motivates such religious acts. The sacrifice that God requires of us has been totally and radically affected by the supreme and totally unmatched sacrifice of God himself in his Son Jesus Christ at the cross. Our sacrifices therefore, whatever form they may take, must be from us the response of gratitude to the prior acts of God in our behalf.

Paul made the same point in his use of the word "sacrifice" in Romans 12:1: "Present yourselves as living sacrifices. This is holy and acceptable." Not our bodies dead upon the altar or wounded through flagellations but able and ready to do God's will as living sacrifices. This is a refreshing and surprising new interpretation of religious sacrifice that Paul has introduced into the whole history of theological dialog.

This is the new logic that stands behind Paul's theology of sacrifice as an act of our discipleship. It is also the intended meaning of Paul's use of the word "sacrifice" in this expression of gratitude to the Philippians because of their kindness toward him. Their acts of love were "living sacrifice" acts of discipleship that flowed out of their experience of God's love. Gratefulness to God for his love is the only religious ritual we need, and as that gratefulness overflows in acts of concrete love toward our neighbor and our brothers and sisters we perform the only sacrificial acts that really make sense now that Christ has fulfilled all of the sacrifices that were a part of the Old Testament drama of the symbols of atonement.

God has accepted their gifts to him that the Philippians had sent to Paul. And now, Paul says, "My God will supply every need of yours according to his riches in glory in Christ Jesus."

God will provide for every need of the Philippians, just as he provided for Paul through the Philippians. God usually uses people to provide for his children. Just as the Philippians gave to Paul, so others will give to the Philippians, perhaps financially, perhaps by providing a listening ear and encouragement, depending on what the needs are.

We must be careful to distinguish between needs and wants. We know very well what we want, but we often do not understand what we truly need. The good work that God has begun in us he will bring to completion, but we will not always understand the way in which he does it. We may need financial losses in order to grow in grace. Or we may need to learn that our time is a gift from God that we must use, not just for ourselves, but also for others; and to teach us this God may put people in our lives who need our time and our undivided attention. Our needs are defined by what God wants us to become, not by what we want to be or do.

It is Paul's custom to take the pen into his own hand from his secretary and write a few final lines of greeting (Gal 6:11; 2 Thess 3:17). He sends greetings from the Christians in Rome who want to be remembered to the Philippians. As Paul makes these last-minute personal notes before Epaphroditus leaves with the letter, he writes, "All the saints greet you," and adds, almost as a footnote, "especially those of Caesar's household."

Perhaps guards from the Roman cohort, the praetorian guard, have become acquainted with Epaphroditus as he served the prisoner Paul. There were speculations in the early church that Paul, during his final imprisonment, had been visited by Roman officials who were themselves troubled on the one side by this remarkable new message about Jesus Christ the Lord and on the other by the increasing decadence and inhumanity of the reign of Emperor Nero. There are accounts in early church writings that Seneca, the brother of Gallio whom Paul had met at Corinth (Acts 18), visited Paul in private, as well as reports of visits by the historian Suetonius.

We cannot conclude such visits from this text, but the fact is that there are persons in the Roman praetorian guard who have become Christians during this time, and they send their Christian greetings. This handful of people in Caesar's household would expand over the years, while the Roman Empire continued on its course toward disintegration.

There is one greater than Caesar, one who shared the cell with Paul, and it is he of whom Paul speaks in his final words to the Philippians. "The grace of the Lord Jesus Christ be with your spirit." Paul invites all men and women of every age to know this Jesus Christ personally and to share with him in his love. We in our generation are included too. The power of this brief letter has crossed over the barriers of time and generations to continue to make sense to each new reader in each new age. It is a letter that deals with the Christian life, its demands, problems and joys. It shows us in word and example what it means to live our lives with Christian integrity—keeping in mind the words of Paul, "Not that I have already obtained this or am already perfect; but I press on to make it my own, because Christ Jesus has made me his own!"

For Reflection:

1. After you finish the final chapter, write down again your definition and description of integrity. (How does it affect you as an individual? You in relation to your family? to the environment? to your church? to your job? You as a citizen with political

and economic responsibilities? Your recreation?)

Now go back to the answer you wrote down at the beginning, after you read the introduction to the book. Compare your two answers.

Afterword

It would be comforting if at the conclusion of this book we could have a simple definition of what integrity is, with some simple guidelines for achieving it. But integrity is not a matter of doing or not doing certain things. It is a way of life. It affects everything we do, from the big, life-changing decisions we must make to the small, incidental encounters in the supermarket. When we try to reduce it to a simple set of rules we have missed the point.

Integrity is somewhat like a jigsaw puzzle. You give your child his or her first "real" jigsaw puzzle, with 500 instead of 36 or 75 pieces. When the child opens the box and dumps all 500 pieces on the table, it doesn't make much sense and the puzzle looks overwhelming. But you start working on the puzzle together because you know that there is a pattern, that there is a way to fit all the pieces together. It will take time, and the child will be tempted to give up, but the picture on the box is the goal, and Mom and Dad, older brothers and sisters are there to help when the going gets tough and patience runs low. But once the puzzle is put together, it all looks so simple and clear.

There are so many pieces in our lives that don't fit that we feel overwhelmed. But the Father is there to work with us, to help us toward completing the pattern. And the closer we get to the goal, the clearer it becomes. As Christians, we know that there is a pattern, that there is a goal: to become the person God intends.

At the heart of integrity lies a center, a focus: Jesus Christ, who loves us and journeys with us. We can begin to integrate our lives when by God's grace we come to realize that we are indeed accepted, fully and unconditionally. Integrity requires facing up to reality, not as we would like it to be or as we pretend it to be, but as it is. Our being accepted by God gives us the freedom to face reality about ourselves, the church and others, without guilt about the past and anxiety about the future. As long as we pretend to be more or less or better or worse than we really are, we cannot have integrity. As long as we idealize ourselves or the church we will spend great amounts of energy trying to keep up the pretense—both to ourselves and to others.

Integrity involves a healthy single-mindedness. "Purity of heart is to will one thing" (Kierkegaard). It involves a refocusing and reintegration of our values and our priorities. Our opportunities to love others usually do not involve great, sacrificial acts but small acts of courtesy and patience. The things we do that others see as major achievements, such as getting a college degree or a major promotion, are relatively minor things when seen from God's perspective. They are cause for gratitude rather than something that boosts our ego and our sense of worth, since our self-worth derives from God's acceptance, not from people's applause.

Integrity has many aspects, and when we make up a list of all that it involves it seems a complex and difficult matter. But the more we understand the gospel, the simpler it becomes. It is not the gospel that is complicated, it is the disharmony in our lives. The more our lives become integrated, the clearer the broad strokes of God's design become.

The road to integrity can be very difficult indeed. Facing reality after we have denied it for many years can be painful—often we cannot face it alone and need the help and support of others. The more sensitive we get to the practical, everyday meaning of the gospel, the more we will realize how far we fall short of true integrity. But we, like Paul, must "press on," reaching toward the goal in spite of our imperfections.

And we must help one another toward integrity. Just as we must learn to live out of the ever-growing awareness of God's grace in Jesus Christ, so we must learn to reflect that grace in our relationship with others, looking at what God has done in their lives rather than at areas where they fall short of full integrity. Integrity is the result of inner healing, of the hand of God touching our inner selves through other people, to make us whole.

Integrity is finally learning what Blaise Pascal meant when he said, "Do great things as though they were small because of Jesus Christ and small things as though they were great because of Jesus Christ."

The grace of the Lord Jesus Christ be with your spirit.

Study Guide to Philippians

Note: Questions are included at the end of each chapter of this book to help you reflect on the material as you read it. The questions listed here comprise a brief study guide to the book of Philippians itself. You may wish to work through Philippians on your own or study it with a friend or a small group.

Study 1   Beginnings of a Friendship   Acts 16

1. Luke narrates the first visit of Paul and his companions to Philippi. What do you learn from this chapter about the atmosphere of the city? How would you describe Philippi?

2. Describe each of the people you meet in the chapter.

3. How does the Christian fellowship begin in Philippi? What are the roles that different people play?

4. Have you had experiences in your own journey of faith similar to the ones Luke narrates here?

Study 2   A Prayer for the People   Philippians 1:1-11

1. When you read the words *peace* and *grace*, what meanings come into your mind?

2. What do you think are some of the needs of the Christians at Philippi on the basis of Paul's prayer for them?

3. What requests in Paul's prayer are especially relevant to your own journey of faith and life?

Study 3   In an Awkward Place   Philippians 1:12-26

1. How would you explain Paul's logic in his statement that because he is in prison, others in the Christian fellowship are more open about sharing the gospel of Christ?

2. What do you learn about Paul's philosophy of life from these few sentences?

3. On the basis of the first twenty-five verses of Philippians, write down everything you know about the convictions of Paul.

Study 4   The Meaning of Courage   Philippians 1:27—2:2

1. What do you think Paul means by his challenge to Christians to live our public lives in keeping with, congruent with, the gospel of Christ?

2. Why would he add, "Don't be startled"?

3. What is the "encouragement in Christ"? List the encouraging things you can think of which are so because of Jesus Christ.

Study 5   An Instinct for the Center   Philippians 2:3-11

1. Paul relates every theme to Jesus Christ. Why?

2. What do you learn about Jesus from the great hymn recorded in these nine verses?

3. What do you learn about yourself in these verses?

Study 6   Light and Life   Philippians 2:12-18

1. Notice the special use of the word *work*. In what two ways does Paul use it? What significance do you attach to the special use of this word?

2. What comes to your mind as Paul uses the words *light* and *life?*

Study 7   People   Philippians 2:19-30; 4:2-3

1. What do you learn from the way Paul talks about the people he mentions in these verses?

2. How can Paul's approach to people help you in your relationships with people in your own life?

3. What are his largest concerns regarding the people he mentions?

4. What are his concerns regarding the church as a whole?

Study 8   Paul's Own Journey   Philippians 3

1. What do you think are some of the reasons Paul decides to narrate his own personal story for the believers at Philippi?

2. Paul reflects on three periods of his life: past, present, future. What does he say about each?

3. In what ways does Paul's personal story help you in your story?

Study 9   Rejoice Together   Philippians 4:1-7

1. Twice Paul gives his exhortation to the church to rejoice. Why do you think he repeats the encouragement to rejoice?

2. Are there reasons why the people in the fellowship might hold back? What holds you back from giving thanks?

3. Why would he urge the fellowship to be moderate? (The word *forbearance* is the Greek word *gentle*.)

4. In what ways is the peace of God a fortress for our lives?

Study 10   The Generosity of God   Philippians 4:8-23

1. When Paul tells his readers to think about these things and to do them, what do you think he means?

2. What is the secret Paul shares with the Philippian believers?

3. Have you noticed throughout the letter ways in which Paul has encouraged the Philippians to stand on their own feet without too much dependence on him? List sentences where you observe Paul's encouragement in that direction.

4. How do you interpret the phrase, "especially those of Caesar's household"?

5. Can you think of instances when the good news of God's love has been discovered in places and times when you would least expect it?

Notes

Introduction
[1]Henri Nouwen, *Making All Things New: An Invitation to the Spiritual Life* (San Francisco: Harper & Row, 1981), pp. 23-24.
[2]*Oxford English Dictionary*, 8:368.
[3]Ibid.
[4]Thomas à Kempis *The Imitation of Christ* 1.1.

Chapter 1: The Road to Integrity
[1]Tacitus *Annals* 90.44.

Chapter 3: The Integrity of the Church
[1]Karl Barth, *Dogmatics in Outline*, trans. G. T. Thomson (New York: Philosophical Library, 1949), p. 10.

Chapter 5: Integrity Under Attack
[1]Marshall Shelley, *Well-Intentioned Dragons* (Waco: Word, 1985), pp. 11-12.

Chapter 6: The Great Choreographer
[1]*Hymns for the Family of God* (Nashville: Paragon Associates, Inc., 1976), #527.
[2]John Calvin, *The Epistles of Paul the Apostle to the Galatians, Ephesians, Philippians and Colossians*, trans. T. H. L. Parker (Grand Rapids, Mich.: Eerdmans, 1965), p. 41.
[3]Dietrich Bonhoeffer, *Letters and Papers from Prison* (New York: Macmillan, 1953), p. 15.

Chapter 7: The Meaning of Congruence
[1]Dietrich Bonhoeffer, *The Cost of Discipleship* (New York: Macmillan, 1963), p. 47.

Chapter 8: Encouragement That Lasts
[1]Dietrich Bonhoeffer, *Life Together*, trans. John W. Doberstein (New York: Harper, 1954), p. 27.

Chapter 9: The Price of Integrity
[1]J. B. Lightfoot, *St. Paul's Epistle to the Philippians* (New York: Macmillan, 1896), p. 38.
[2]Ibid., p. 39.
[3]Augustine *Confessions*.
[4]Barth, *Dogmatics in Outline*, p. 66.
[5]Ibid.

Chapter 14: Purity of Heart
[1]C. F. D. Moule, *Epistle of Paul the Apostle to the Philippians* (Cambridge, England: Cambridge University Press, 1890), p. 99.
[2]Ibid., p. 117.
[3]Barmen Declaration, *Book of Confession* (Presbyterian Church [U.S.A.]).

Chapter 15: Models of Hope
[1]See Moule, *Epistle of Paul the Apostle to the Philippians*, p. 102.

Chapter 16: The Gospel for People in Stress
[1]Bonhoeffer, *The Cost of Discipleship*, p. 85.

Chapter 17: Focused Integrity
[1]Karl Barth, *The Epistle to the Philippians*, trans. James W. Leitch (Richmond, Va.: John Knox, 1962), p. 120.
[2]Lightfoot, *St. Paul's Epistle to the Philippians*, p. 158.

Chapter 18: The Generosity of Love
[1]Bonhoeffer, *Letters and Papers from Prison*, p. 17.